11-62

A Study of Black Adoption Families:
A Comparison of a Traditional
and a Quasi-Adoption Program

Elizabeth A. Lawder, D.S.W.
Janet L. Hoopes, Ph.D.
Roberta G. Andrews, M.S.S.
Katherine D. Lower, Ph.D.
Susan Y. Perry, M.S.S.

Copyright 1971
Child Welfare League of America, Inc.
Library of Congress
Catalog Card Number: 71-170922
ISBN Number: 0-87868-089-6

FOREWORD

The greatest need in the adoption field is for demonstrations of ways in which the doors to adoption can be opened for black children of all ages and degrees of risk.

Increased opportunities for adoption benefit not only the children who have been surrendered, such as those described in this study. These opportunities also benefit the biological mothers who have wished adoption for their children but have feared that surrender would not result in placement, as well as the biological mothers who are not permitted by agencies to consider surrender. As still another benefit, parenthood is happily made possible for couples who at first were not ready to undertake it.

The program reported in this monograph is noteworthy for several reasons. It has definitely offered a new avenue to adoption of black children. It has devoted its resources to innovation within the black community on behalf of inracial adoption. And it is an example of the kind of adventurous work that has prepared the case for subsidized adoption and its enactment into law in a number of states. The Child Welfare League is pleased to bring this program to the attention of the field.

Carl Schoenberg
Director of Publications
Child Welfare League of America

ACKNOWLEDGMENTS

This report is the third prepared as a result of adoption research undertaken by the Children's Aid Society of Pennsylvania and Bryn Mawr College. The initial grants for this study were made by the Seybert Institution and the Samuel S. Fels Foundation. Subsequent support was given by the U.S. Children's Bureau, Department of Health, Education and Welfare, under grant #86-P-900039-3-01.

Many individuals contributed to this study, especially Edmund A. Sherman, Ph.D., who was a member of the research team and an author of the first two studies and a consultant on this one. The interviewers were: Douglas C. Freeler, M.S.W., Roshan R. Malva, M.S.W., Robert Morgan, M.A., Penelope A. Purnell, M.S.W., and Patricia S. Schogel, M.S.W. The psychologists were: Mary Fox, M.A., and Lafayette Powell, Ph.D. The observers were: Armond Aserinsky, M.A., Carol Aserinsky, B.S., Robert L. Dutton, M.S.W., and Susan Levett Shilling, M.S.W. The independent rater for the interviews was Evalyn M. Strickler, M.S.W.; the rater of records was Norma K. Craythorne, M.S.W.

Secretarial assistance was provided by Marjorie Maytrott and Gwendolyn Powell.

The research team expresses appreciation to all those who contributed funds and time to this study and to the adoption parents and children who participated in it.

TABLE OF CONTENTS

1

The Program

The quasi-adoption service of the Children's Aid Society of Pennsylvania is one of the many efforts in the child welfare field to provide stable, permanent homes for black children. Its creation in 1964 was the culmination of 15 years of experimentation in attempting to achieve a higher number of adoption placements for black children. As long ago as 1949 it was predicted by the Health and Welfare Council in Philadelphia that the needs of dependent black children would reach crisis proportions because their numbers were beginning to exceed placement resources. The demographic changes within this urban area have added urgency to the earlier warning.

In the 1950s the Children's Aid Society launched intensive recruitment drives to attract more black adoption families, as did other similar agencies. As a part of this overall effort, staff attitudes were examined and procedures were carefully scrutinized to discover whether there were internal deterrents that might prevent potential black adoption parents from applying. The objective was to find ways, through greater understanding on the agency's part, to increase the confidence of these families in taking the necessarily formal legal steps that are a part of adoption.

Every avenue in the community was used to interpret the child's need and to inform black families regarding the nature of adoption. Public meetings were held, staff members met with church and civic organizations and the public media were heavily employed. This interpretive effort was an important first step. Although adoption placements of black children increased only modestly, the families who responded became more and more competent as parents. The circumstances of those responding reflected better-than-usual educational and employment status.

By the early 1960s, however, the crisis prediction had become a reality and it was necessary to discover a method for widening the range of potential parents. This was necessary not only to increase the numbers of adoption parents, but to provide for children whose abilities, temperament and needs varied greatly.

A survey was made of all families applying to us for children, including both potential adoption and foster families. We identified a group of families who were interested in foster children but who expressed a preference for a child who would grow up with them as a member of the family. These families said they could not endure the heartache of separating from a child in whom they had invested so much. When the possibility of adoption was explored with these families, various reasons, economic and psychological, were given for preferring foster care. Among the reasons given for ambivalence about adoption, financial uncertainty and anxiety about legal responsibility for the child predominated.

Economic deterrents were real enough; a majority of the families had lower incomes and more debts and family obligations than traditional adoption families, black or white. Evaluating the psychological resistance to adoption was more difficult. We had noted that foster parents a few weeks or months after the placement of a young child began to inquire about the possibility of adopting him. We wondered whether these families needed actual experience with a child to decide whether he was developing well, was compatible with the family and was accepted by relatives and friends. There appeared to be less trust in the agency's selection of the child for them than was true of traditional adoption families. Many of these parents had experienced directly or indirectly the "informal adoption" of the children of relatives, and some had been brought up themselves under such an arrangement. It was hypothesized that this group of families, because of these economic, sociological and psychological realities and experience, might respond to an arrangement that met their emotional needs and commitments but that provided a sharing of responsibility with the agency.

In 1964 the quasi-adoption service became one of the earliest formalized subsidized adoption plans in the country. The final step was taken to meet a crisis in the Philadelphia community resulting from a back-up of black infants in the city hospital. This situation came to a head because mothers, unable to care for their newborns, left them behind in the safe hands of the hospital. This immediate dilemma was easily solved and the new program opened its doors to young black children, whatever their location, needing permanent families.

The Philadelphia Department of Public Welfare supported and encouraged the establishment of this service. The department agreed to a purchase-of-care arrangement which continues to the present. The United Fund provided a grant for initial expenses. The combination of public and voluntary funding and cooperation brought into being this new service for black children.

The usual recruitment devices were expanded to include ad hoc meetings with small groups of black parents who had already adopted children through the Children's Aid Society. They not only advised the agency on the most effective ways of reaching potential quasi-adoption parents, but discussed with their friends, church and civic groups this new way of caring for young black children. These groups helped in two significant ways. First, they enlarged the staff's understanding of the attitudes of quasi-adoption applicants. Second, in their recruitment efforts, these families went straight to the target population. There is little doubt that the cooperation of our own adoption families was a significant component in bringing families to us.

The design of the quasi-adoption service was carefully constructed to interest the group of potential parents who had expressed so clearly their wish for a permanent relationship with a young placed child. Financial support of the child was considered by the agency to be a key ingredient not only because of the practical importance to the family, but because it symbolized a shared responsibility for the child in a specific, well-defined and nonthreatening way. Money was available for the child's board, clothing and daily expenses; the agency provided medical care for the child and legal expenses at time of adoption, if needed. Quasi-adoption parents had the choice of accepting all or part of the child's expenses, with the agency expressing a preference for continuing medical supervision until adoption. Most families chose full support until the decision to adopt was made. The court required that the adopting parents assume full support prior to the legal completion of adoption, a period that usually spanned 2 to 3 months or more.

The supervision of the child's placement was, of course, a matter of legal and professional responsibility. Added to this obligation, it was hypothesized that the quasi-adoption families would need more help than traditional adoption families with problems of planning for the family, child rearing and communication about adoption. The staff, therefore, adopted a broader approach to the entire family and was ready to offer consultation on family problems as well as support in decisions affecting family life.

Basic requirements for the acceptance of quasi-adoption families by the agency were flexible and related to the expectation that the length of the relationship would be longer than is characteristic of traditional adoption placements. The applicants were expected to be a married couple, between their mid-20s and early 50s, who evidenced verbally and nonverbally a warm and firm commitment to being parents to a nonrelated child. It was expected also that the parents would possess the potential of providing adequately for the child economically and emotionally throughout his dependent years, and that they would have some community ties and a respect for appropriate education for the child.

The agency anticipated that some families would have marginal housing, that the man of the house might have less job security and be less well paid than traditional adoption fathers. Also it was thought that some marriages would not have been legalized and that there might be for some parents a record of arrest and conviction. The staff was aware that in the family situations described, marital problems could easily center around boredom and feelings of depression and loneliness for the wife. Also, experience indicated that some of these husbands were overly dependent upon their wives and the advent of a child might threaten to decrease their gratifications.

The approach to the family study was in the spirit of understanding a life experience that included a mixture of success and problem. The evaluation required a well-balanced understanding and an estimate of how successfully the couple had overcome adversity, how ready they were to offer a relatively stable family life to a child.

Procedures were set up whereby each inquiry from a potential quasi-adoption family was given immediate attention. Within a few days contact was made and an appointment scheduled within 2 weeks either in the office or in the home, depending upon the applicants' preference. The family study was completed within 4 to 6 weeks, if the timing was acceptable to the family. At the start of the service, few families had to wait more than a week or so for the child of their choice. The agency studied waiting children concurrently with the family studies and prepared them for placement.

At the inception of the quasi-adoption program, training sessions with the staff were held at which service objectives and methods were discussed. Risks were evaluated and decisions shared. These sessions then became an ongoing way of marshaling all agency resources to support and develop this new service to black children. As an outgrowth of the discussions, specific practical ways of helping families evolved and became a basic part of the program. These families asked for tangible assistance; i.e., help in applying for a new job, instructions regarding enrollment in Get Set or Head Start, encouragement to join in community activities, reassurance regarding a move to better quarters. A few families wanted information about budgeting, insurance, and payment of debts. For the most part, families developed a feeling of comfort with the staff and considerable freedom in communication. This interchange was greatly enhanced because in most cases the caseworker who began with the family continued with them through the family study, placed the child and continued on afterward with them. There is no question but that the continuity of this relationship was a plus factor for both the family and child.

As to the agency's work with the child, the same conditions obtained in the study and placement of the child as exist in traditional adoption placements. A social, medical and psychological assessment of the child was made, as was a study of his background to the extent possible. A termination of the rights of the natural parents was obtained in order to make possible permanent placement with the quasi-adoption parents. The same methods employed in traditional placements in selecting compatible children and parents were used in the new service. Therefore, quasi-adoption parents had the same assurance as all other adoption parents that the agency's total services were available to help child and family grow together compatibly. Furthermore, they were assured that should they delay in deciding upon adoption, the agency would not remove the child for that reason. Should the family decide against adoption, they could be reclassified as permanent foster parents and continue to receive payment for the child's expenses.

The majority of applicant families were accepted, although more were rejected than is generally the case in adoption. Some of those who were accepted had tasks to accomplish before placement. For example, some couples were assisted in accomplishing a legal marriage. Others were helped to investigate old police and prison records and to work through feelings that remained. Casework help was given to several couples who needed to ventilate and settle differences, mainly in the area of unrealistic demands upon each other. The staff was impressed with the resilience and motivation of the families.

As the quasi-adoption program developed, the agency became interested in studying the likenesses and differences between these families and traditional adoption families and in evaluating adoption outcome. Clinically both groups demonstrated adaptibility and the ability to cope with reality problems. The agency valued these qualities as essential to successful parenting. In two previous studies[1] it was clearly shown that the ability to cope with life as it is was directly related to the outcome of adoption. There were, however, striking differences in the social circumstances of the families previously studied and those in the current study. The social climate and forces affecting black families were actively changing. All quasi-adoption and traditional adoption black families experienced improved opportunities between 1964 and the time of the study. Had family values changed? Did any such changes affect adoption outcome? Were there specific problematic areas in the placement? Were black parents uneasy or relatively comfortable about discussing the child's adoption status? It was hoped that this study of a selected group of families would be a step toward understanding the values of these adoption families who in combination offered an expanded opportunity for parentless black children.

There is no doubt that those social workers who studied the families and placed these children, the research interviewers and the team who spent many hours studying tapes, admired the qualities of warmth and unity characteristic of these families. The feeling for the families, whose strength was born of hardship, undoubtedly affected the ratings by the research team. It was impossible not to respond positively to families whose attitudes were conveyed symbolically by the response of one adoption father. Asked what he liked about family life, he said, "All of it."

References

1. Elizabeth A. Lawder *et al., A Followup Study of Adoptions: Post-Placement Functioning of Adoption Families, Vol. I* (New York: Child Welfare League of America, 1969); Janet L. Hoopes *et al., A Followup Study of Adoptions: Post-Placement Functioning of Adopted Children, Vol. II* (New York: Child Welfare League of America, 1970).

2

Methodology

A. Purpose

This study is a further extension of research reported in *A Followup Study of Adoptions: Post-Placement Functioning of Adoption Families* and *A Followup Study of Adoptions: A Study of the Adjustment of Adopted Children*. The earlier studies, begun in 1960, were limited to white families legally adopting white children between 1950-1957. There were two primary reasons for restricting the earlier studies to white families; first, the number of black adoption families in those earlier years was small, and, second, it was thought that black families, at that time and as a group, differed from white families in many socioeconomic and cultural ways. Black families adopting through the Children's Aid Society in the 1950s were less well off educationally and economically than white adoption families.

In the mid-1960s, the agency began the quasi-adoption service already described. Traditional adoption and the new service provided a way of selecting a broad range of families to serve a variety of children in need of permanent homes. A systematic study of these two approaches to adoption should yield information useful in adoption practice.

The broad objectives of this study are to compare family and child functioning in the two groups and to study outcome of adoption within each group.

B. Design

This study begins at the point at which husband and wife apply for a child through either the quasi-adoption program or through the conventional program. The psychosocial functioning of these two adults as individuals and as marital partners can be broadly conceived of as independent variables in the design. From an assessment of this

6

functioning, the general intent is to predict or explain "adoption outcome," the dependent variable. The child, however, becomes an intervening factor in this scheme. The family unit has been elaborated in an interactional sense by the placement of the child. Therefore, the effect of the child's placement both on the family homeostasis and on the child himself has been evaluated. The evaluation of "outcome," then, includes not only parental functioning but also child functioning. Finally, there is an additional intervening factor in the form of "agency service." It was believed that quasi-adoption families would have received more service than traditional adoption families.

Schematically, the design flows as follows:

Independent Variables	Intervening Factors	Dependent Variables
Mother & father ⟶	Child ⟶ Agency service ⟶	Outcome measures
(individual & marital		(parental function-
functioning)		ing & child adjust-
		ment)

C. Measures

Several scales were constructed to measure the designated variables. A search of the literature yielded few measures considered appropriate for this population. Many of the available scales have been standardized on and used with a white middle-class population. Since it was important to obtain the participation and cooperation of as many families as possible, and since it also was important to keep the interview with these families non-structured and free-flowing, complicated and difficult scales and schedules were avoided. All of the data were obtained verbally. Some of the schedules were adapted from the previous study on white adoptions.

1. Data on Parents

a. Certain demographic data were obtained on these families at the time they applied for adoption. Information was also available on the couples' preferences about the type of child they would want, e.g., color, intelligence, health, personality factors. These data are recorded in the case record, and a data sheet was used to collect the information for this study. (See Case Record Data Sheet, Appendix C.)*

b. From the Schematic Chart for the design of the study it is apparent that it was necessary to obtain measures of the relevant variables. One of the theoretical considerations of this study was the effect of childhood deprivation in the lives of parents on their child-rearing capacity. Clinical impressions indicated that many of these parents had experienced some degree of deprivation in early life. For as full a picture as possible, it seemed important to record not only pertinent obtainable facts, but the individual's feelings about past economic and emotional deprivation.

A study by Banks and Cappon[1] served as a point of reference in constructing Schedule V, titled "Early Experiences Which May Have Affected Current Child-Rearing Attitudes" (see Appendix). Some items from the questionnaire used by Banks and Cappon were adapted for use and additional items were included. The items considered indicative of feelings of deprivation are as follows:

---

*The appendices are not published in this volume, but are available on request from *The Children's Aid Society of Pennsylvania,* 311 South Juniper St., Philadelphia, Pa. 19107.

Remembering childhood as moderately unhappy.
Remembering childhood as very unhappy.
Remembering insufficient food as a child.
Remembering insufficient clothing as a child.
Remembering insufficient housing as a child.
Growing up with only one parent.
Loss of mother in early years (0-5 years).
Loss of father in early years (0-5 years).
Loss of both parents in early years (0-5 years).
Living with another relative — grandparent, aunt, uncle, etc.
Living in a foster home, shelter, hospital, etc.
Moving from family to family two or more times.
Growing up separated from siblings.
Mother or substitute parent did not want or hated client.
Father or substitute parent did not want or hated client.
Client feels neutral toward or hated mother or substitute parent.
Client feels neutral toward or hated father.
Parents of client did not love one another.
Client feels he or she never had much in life.
Client feels he or she better hang on to all he or she can get.
Client feels nobody cared about him or her.
Client feels he or she does not want child to go through what he or or she did with
      parents.

The number of items checked by the interviewer was tallied for each parent inter-viewed. It was assumed that a combination of a substantial number of these items might have a negative influence on parents' current child-rearing attitudes.

c. It was hypothesized that satisfying experiences later in a person's life might modify the effects and feelings of earlier deprivation. In addition, other persons outside the nuclear family might significantly influence an individual's emotional growth after the crucial early years.[2,3] Schedule VI (see Appendix) was constructed to elicit data on experiences and persons that may have supported in adult life the growth and ego func-tioning of these parents. Not all experiences and persons may have had a positive effect, so neutral and negative categories were also included. The hypothesis was that the better functioning families would describe a number of experiences and persons that had in-fluenced their lives positively, while the poorer functioning families would describe fewer, or more negative influences. A simple tally of the number of experiences and persons with a positive influence was used as a measure of ego strength that might have counteracted negative childhood factors.

d. It was thought that, given fairly healthy ego functioning and sense of identity in the two parents, a successful marriage would expand the social and emotional functioning of each partner. The schedule devised to measure marital functioning was adapted from scales included in a study by the Community Service Society of New York.[4] The scale dealing with perception of marital satisfaction was adapted and scaled as seen in Schedule VII (see Appendix). Several aspects of the marital relationship were considered important to a total perception of marital satisfaction. These were: the affectional aspects of the

8

relationship; sex relations; finances; marital organization, and communication with each other. Suggested interview questions to elicit the data for rating Schedule VII are listed in the Appendix. The ratings are scaled on a 1 to 5 ordinal scale, with 5 indicating maximum satisfaction and 1, low satisfaction.

2. Data on the Child Placed

Factors related to the child placed with a family affect the total family situation. These factors include both constitutional and experiential variables. Current research has demonstrated that normal or well adapted child-parent functioning depends not only on the parenting given by each parent with his or her unique background experiences, but on the individual makeup of each child.[5]

a. Constitutional factors: Data were available on what might be considered constitutional factors, such as mental illness or mental retardation in the background, the kind of prenatal care received by the mother, and the birth history. These data were found in the case records, and were rated by the research individual who read the case record data. The items are included in that data sheet in Appendix C. The items measuring constitutional factors in a gross fashion are as follows: mother or father mentally limited, mother or father mentally ill, complications or illness during pregnancy, presence or absence of prenatal care, term of pregnancy, Apgar rating, complications of delivery and birth weight. At the time of the developmental examination, the psychologist rated activity level, mood, attention span, and developmental level. Items considered problematic or negative for constitutional makeup of the child were rated 2, positive information was rated 0, and questionable background information or mild problems were rated 1. It was possible, therefore, to obtain a maximum score of 30 on the fifteen items relating to constitution (see Case Record Data, Appendix C).

b. Experiential factors: The items describing early living experiences are child shelter experience, overt neglect or abuse, number of foster homes, feeling tone of the foster mother (warm vs. hostile), feeding problems, frequent illness, age at adoption placement. These experiences were likewise rated 2, 1, or 0, so that 14 was the possible total score on the seven items dealing with early living experiences (see Case Record Data, Appendix C).

3. Agency Service Data

Because of our belief that quasi-adoption couples were older, and had had fewer educational and job opportunities than the couples in the traditional program, we hypothesized that they would need more service in regard to problems in caring for a young child, and to improvement of family circumstances. In addition quasi-adoption families might not begin parenting experiences at so high a level of adult functioning as traditional adoption families. This was assumed because of the possible influence of the lower educational and economic level of the quasi families. The agency offered both financial and supportive social services to these quasi-adoption families. It was presumed that these families, then, might function at the level of the traditional adoption families through this service factor. Some measure was needed, therefore, to compare the quasi and traditional families in terms of the relative frequency of types and kinds of service provided. Service data were collected directly from agency records. The operational definition of a service in this study is the following: *A service is any recorded social work activity that falls within a defined service category.* Social work activity refers to the recorded actions of the assigned agency social worker in working with, or in behalf of, the family or child who is placed. The defined service categories are as follows:

Family functioning — Help related to personal and individual functioning within the family unit: carrying parental responsibility for care and guidance of children; improving parent-child, marital and sibling relationships; dealing with special stresses disruptive of family life, such as overburdening of one or more members.

Physical functioning — Help to child or adult in obtaining medical care, nursing services, home health aids, medicines; also, arrangements for transporting children to and from clinics, hospitals, physicians' offices.

Financial functioning — Help in regard to money management, use of financial resources, debt management, budgeting and purchasing.

Social and community functioning — Help in maintaining or improving social relationships outside the nuclear family in community life; encouragement and support in beginning or maintaining social, civic, religious and recreational contacts and activities.

Maintaining home — Help related to improving or maintaining physical aspects of a house or apartment, and improving homemaking skills by use of homemakers.

Vocational functioning — Help with adjustment and behavior related to employment, and assistance in changing employment or improving opportunities.

Educational services — (a)   Help related to use of educational or training opportunities such as adult education, community training and retraining; also help on adjustment or behavior in school. (b)   Help related to adoption education for both the parents and child.

Legal adoption services — Assistance with relinquishment, abandonment, and final adoption proceedings.

Financial assistance — Payment of child's expenses in part or completely, including such items as board, clothing, medical care and legal expenses for adoption.

Service data were collected from case records up to the closing of the case after adoption was consummated, or up to the final date of the data collection of the study (September 1, 1968) if adoption had not been completed. Two basic service factors were identified: type of social work activity, and the service category into which the activity fell. The discrete recorded casework activity is the basic unit for counting a single service. For example, if a caseworker recorded that a child was referred to a pediatric clinic for an examination, this would count as a service under the category of "Physical functioning."

In addition to the classification of services by types, there was a classification of the methods by which the services were provided. Gordon Hamilton's classification of treatment methods was modified for use.[6] The three basic types of casework treatment outlined in Professor Hamilton's scheme were: administration of a practical service; environmental manipulation; direct interviewing treatment. The modification of this scheme and definitions used are as follows (see Appendix E):

Administration of a practical service includes any casework activity that assists the client (family) to choose or use a social resource. "Social resource" is interpreted to mean the agency's own resources (e.g., providing a clothing grant for a child), as well as any other agency with appropriate services. Thus, the cited example of a child referred to a pediatric clinic for examination was classified under "administration of a practical service," because the clinic is considered a "social resource."

Supportive treatment is essentially a method of apprising a client of factors, both psychological and environmental, that impede his maximal functioning. The techniques on an educational level include the giving of advice and practical information; on a psychological level they include reassurance, encouragement and ventilation within the framework of a warm, sympathetic, positive relationship between client and social worker.

Direct treatment as defined by Hamilton is ". . . a series of interviews carried on with the purpose of inducing or reinforcing attitudes favorable to maintenance of emotional equilibrium, to making constructive decisions, and to growth or change."[7] In identifying this process from case record material the reader looked for conscious (recorded) use of relationship by the social worker to bring about change in the situation.

The goal of adoption is the selection of parents and children who together form a relatively healthy family unit. Supervision of such placements is a supportive process to facilitate family functioning. Hence the category of direct treatment was of dubious applicability in this study but was retained in the event it should show up to a limited extent in the case record.

4. Parent Functioning

The final area of data collection dealt with the current functioning of these adoption families and their adopted children. The outcome of adoption measures on parent functioning and child adjustment are the dependent variables against which all the other variables were correlated. Data obtained on outcome of adoption fulfilled the objectives of the study, which were to determine differences between the two groups of families, and also to describe parental functioning and child adjustment in the two types of families.

In the study on white adoption families, the home interviews collected data on parent attitudes toward parenthood in general, and adoption parenthood specifically. In this study replication of these data was considered important. The schedule used in the previous research was modified slightly, and included the following subsections: satisfaction in parental role; acceptance of adoptive role; effectiveness of communication concerning adoption; parental warmth and affection; agreement on issues in child rearing. This latter item was new. Omitted from this scale in this study was the item on marital satisfaction, since it was included in the separate Marital Functioning scale. Schedule IV in the Appendix lists these items and the Rating Scale, which was completed by the interviewer following the home interview with the family. Separate ratings were obtained on the attitudes of both mother and father. A score of 5 indicates an optimum level of functioning, and a score of 1, a low level. An average of the ratings on the five components of this scale provided an overall rating for parental functioning.

5. Child Functioning

The test of adoption outcome is the adjustment of the child. Observations on the child himself were considered crucial, and the study was designed to include assessment of the child by a psychologist. However, in addition to the observations made on the child, interview data were obtained on the parents' perception of the child's adjustment.

a. Parent's description of child: The descriptive material obtained from both parents concerning the child's behavior is scaled in Schedule III. The areas rated were: aggressive/passive; dependent/independent; defiant/compliant; destructive/careful; responsive to other children/withdrawn; greedy/fussy about food; fearful/reckless; jealous/accepting of siblings. It was important to scale these items so that the optimum point of adjustment indicated a balance between extremes of behavior. For example, in the item dealing with aggression vs. passivity, the optimum level of behavior should indicate normal assertiveness with occasional temper and outbursts, and a general balance between passive and aggressive behavior. As can be seen in Schedule III, the items were divided into two sections, and the rater rated the child, based on the parental interview, on either one or the other half of the item. Five was considered a midpoint for the item, and the child might deviate to either the aggressive or passive side. A rating of 1, therefore, represented either an overly aggressive or an overly passive child, both of which were considered deviant. An average score for the eight items was obtained from both mother's and father's rating.

b. Problem checklist: A list of problem behaviors was adapted from the study on white adoption families. This problem checklist was filled out by the home interviewer from the parents' report. The interviewer judged whether the problem was mild, moderate or severe. A tally of the total number of problems was obtained, as well as a breakdown by category of mild, moderate or severe. This score was an additional indication of the child's adjustment.

c. Testing Session: Each child was seen in the office when his parents came in for the office interview. The test session with the child dealt with three aspects: 1) intellectual development; 2) emotional functioning, and 3) interaction between child and parent.

1) Measurement of intelligence — All of the children were measured on the Stanford Binet Form L-M, 1960 revision.

2) Measurement of emotional functioning — An adaptation of the Structural Doll Play Test by David Lynn[8] was devised for this group of children. The cardboard dolls and cardboard settings were replaced by three-dimensional material. The Flagg plastic, flexible play dolls, which come in a family group of black people, were used. The settings from the doll play that were used were: crib or bed choice; bottle or glass choice; fighting; separation; misbehavior; toilet/potty choice, and nightmare or night fears. Three-dimensional furniture appropriate to the size of the plastic dolls was purchased. This included a baby crib, a single child-size bed, a plastic bottle, a cup, a small potty chair, and a double bed for both parents, to be used in the "night fears" setting. Instructions for the doll play were taken from the Lynn test (see Appendix).

The doll play observations were scored for object choice, whether mature or immature, and also for choice of parent in troublesome or fearful or dependent situations. There are limited normative data on doll play observations for lower - to middle-class black children in this age range. Lynn found that white nursery-age children still tend to make some immature object choices. Sears's[9] study of middle- and working-class white families indicated that the working-class families generally expressed more frustration at dependent behavior and tended to be stricter and more punitive in their handling of this behavior than middle-class families. If the child's selection of the object represented his feelings about "not being a baby," the doll play situation might then provide some measure of his push toward independence and might also reflect parental attitude toward dependence/independence. Object choice can also be related, of course, to other factors described and measured in the study, such as age and intelligence of the child, early history of the child, and factors in the parents' background.

The literature has indicated the predominance of the mother in the black family. If true, this group of children could be expected to choose the mother more frequently in the various situations of the doll play. However, other theoretical constructs pointed toward the choosing of the father by the girl child and the mother by the boy child. The Freudian concept of the oedipal period through which most of these children were passing supports this kind of choice.

Sears's study also pointed out distinct class differences in the kinds of discipline used; for example, lower-class families tended to use physical punishment and depriva- tion of privileges more frequently than middle-class families, who used withdrawal of love. In the current study it was possible to rate the child's verbalizations on the doll play according to whether they perceived the parent as punitive or not in those items involving bad or dependent behavior on the part of the child. Five of the seven items could be rated this way. If the child indicated such punitiveness in all five instances, or four of the five, his perception of the parent was rated as punitive. If, on the other hand, he per- ceived the parent as supportive in all five instances, or four of the five, then his perception of the parent was rated as warm and supportive. It was planned, then, to relate the child's perception of the parent to the interviewer's rating of the parents' warmth and affection toward the child and to social class. Perception of the parent was also related to other child factors, such as intelligence, age and the number of problems noted by the psychol- ogist. The doll play situation, therefore, presented an opportunity to obtain some des- criptive normative behavior on this group of black children, and also provided an oppor- tunity for comparison with different factors in the child and parent background and in the current family functioning.

3) Measurement of parent-child interaction — Some of the most valuable information about how a child and parent are relating and adapting can be observed in interaction between the mother and child or father and child. There have been previous models for studying parent-child interaction, such as the work of Merrill,[10] Rosen,[11] and Zunich.[12] In such situations, parent and child are usually observed together in a task set up by the examiner. An attempt was made to construct an interaction situation in this study that might provide information concerning the following:

Warmth and affection
In the previous adoption study of white families, one of the most important factors in outcome of the adoption was the presence of warmth and affection manifested by the parent for the child. The home interview provided some data on this variable (see Schedule IV). The interaction situation might provide an opportunity to observe the parents actually demonstrating such warmth and affection. It was hypothesized that if the parents felt this way toward the child, they would positively and actively en- courage a child in a task. The negative aspect of this might be manifested in derogation and discouragement of the child in such a task.

Achievement motivation
The earlier study of white adoption families found that parents valued the child's

achievement highly, but that parental expectation sometimes limited the child's independence in choices toward that end. Some studies have demonstrated that independence training and achievement motivation are related.[13] In these preschool children, one might be able to observe how parents encouraged independence in an ego task. If a task were selected within the capacity of the child, the child could be expected to work independently on it. Also, if the child were oriented to task completion and had been encouraged at home in this way, he should keep working on such a task and probably ask for a minimal amount of help. If, on the other hand, he were overly dependent upon parental direction and hence had not incorporated much motivation to achieve, he might continuously seek help or leave the task unless redirected by the parent to complete it. The parents' response, in turn, might yield data on their overcontrol and direction of a child's behavior; or on the other hand, their passivity or lack of encouragement toward task completion. Either behavior might discourage independence on the part of the child.

In this study, a one-way screen and microphone setup provided an opportunity to observe the child in an ego-task situation with either one parent or both parents present. The task selected for this observation was a block-building one that had no right or wrong scoring and that could be performed adequately by all children in the age range 3 through 6. The Blockhead Game was used. The psychologist illustrated how a tower could be built of the crazy-shape blocks, urged the child to make as tall a tower as possible before he returned, and then left the parent and child alone in the room for a 4-minute period.

Observers were instructed to check certain behavior during this interaction situation. The parent was observed for nonverbal, verbal, controlling or passive behavior in relation to the child. All but the last category included both a positive and negative dimension.

Nonverbal negative behavior included: pushing or forcing the child, showing signs of annoyance or irritation.

Nonverbal positive behavior including: helping him with the task, putting an arm around him, smiling, nodding "yes."

Verbal negative behavior included: comments such as "You're wrong," "Why can't you do it?"

Verbal positive behavior included: "Go ahead," "Try it," "That's right," "Do it yourself."

Controlling behavior was rated if the parent verbally directed the child either negatively ("Not that block") or positively ("Put the block there," "Try it over here").

Passive behavior — A pretest of the interaction situation showed that some parents did not interact much with the child. Hence the category of "passive" behavior was added to the scoring. It included either ignoring the child or merely sitting and looking interested, but neither talking or helping or controlling.

The child was observed and rated on whether he worked on the task; left the field, i.e., played with something else; asked for help; worked autonomously (asked no help); or actively refused to do the task (see Instruction for Observers and Score Sheet for Interaction in the Appendix).

d. Psychologist's ratings of problems in the child: Following the psychological testing session, the psychologist wrote a brief report summarizing impressions about the child as he or she related in the test situation or as the parent reported in the interview with the psychologist following the testing. The number of problems noted by the psychologist were used as an overall measure of the child's functioning. There was no other way to obtain an overall score on the child, since the various tasks were separate. The problems noted by the psychologist are categorized as follows:

CRITERIA FOR RATING PSYCHOLOGIST'S REPORTS

1. Hyperactivity: Child does not stay seated, moves quickly from one thing to another.

2. Hard to Control: Examiner finds that verbal commands are ignored and must be repeated, or physical restraint must be used.

3. Inattentive: Although child stays seated and works along with examiner, he seems not to listen to instructions. He may appear to have difficulty understanding examiner.

4. Unhappy: Child's mood is negative; includes difficulty in separating from parents, anxiety, sadness, hostility, shyness, fearfulness.

5. Speech Difficulties: Stuttering, unclear articulation, etc.

6. Counseling Suggested by Examiner: Examiner must strongly indicate that parents should set up an appointment for professional guidance. Comments by the examining psychologist to the effect that agency services are available if needed in the future should not be scored.

7. Parental Reports of Problems: Parent recounts present-day problems with child. Do not include passive agreement with examiner, who may have pointed out what he thinks is a problem. "Problems" include school difficulty, poor peer relationships, destructiveness, disobedience, unhappiness, toilet-training difficulties, etc.

8. Physical Handicap or Disfiguration: Includes severe eye problems, weight problems, gross motor problems.

9. Examiner "Feels" Something Is Wrong: But can't quite put his finger on it. Do not use this category if you have scored anything in categories 1, 2, 3, 4 or 5.

The total number of problems noted could range as high as 8. Some children were expected to have no problems; others were expected to fall between the two extremes.

Reliability of the Instruments

Reliability was computed on Schedules III, IV, V, VI, VII, and the Interaction and Doll Play situation for the children. An independent rater listened to the tapes of interview schedules, and made her own ratings of the interview data. Twenty tapes were rated and reliability coefficients were computed using percentages and the Index Order of Association. With the exception of one item on the child's behavior (defiant/compliant), all items demonstrated significant reliability. In the Interaction Situation and Doll Play, two observers recorded the behavior. Interobserver agreement was statistically significant at the .01 level. Since Schedules I and II contain descriptive data rather than judgmental, no reliability was computed on these. Reliability of the service data was computed during the pretest period with this scale. Two caseworkers reading the record and rating the service type and method independently agreed with each other in a statistically significant fashion.

D. Sample

The chronological starting point for selection of the sample was determined by the experimental quasi-adoption program that began in 1964. The basic population included all families in both the quasi and traditional program with whom children had been placed between September 1, 1964, and September 1, 1968. There were 158 families, 78 quasi-adoption and 80 traditional adoption. Since the plan was to study both the children and parents, consideration was given to the age of the children in the sample. In any study of young children there are great differences in functioning due to age, and also difficulties in the selection of test measures applicable to all ages. It was decided to exclude those children whose speech was not sufficiently developed to use standard intelligence measures. Therefore, no children less than 3 years old were studied. Although the quasi-adoption program was new, there were some children who were older when placed, and were more than 6 years of age at the time of this study. Since these children had already begun school, it was decided to exclude those children who had had more than minimal exposure to influence outside the home. The study population, therefore, was restricted to families with children in the age range 3 through 6. One hundred twenty-five of the 158 families met this criterion. Two of these families lived outside the Philadelphia area and were excluded for practical reasons. The remaining 123 families were randomized, and from this pool 50 quasi-adoption families and 50 traditional adoption families were selected for study. Letters were sent to these families asking their participation in the study. When the home interviews started, some families refused; other families could not be located. Additional letters were sent as refusals or nonlocatable families could not be contacted. Eventually, all 123 families were contacted by letter.

The total number of families seen in some phase of the study was 76, 39 quasi- and 37 traditional adoption. The 76 families included a total of 82 children. Since each child represents a separate adoption, the child sample is the basis sample for data analysis.

Seventy-six families were interviewed at home. In order to complete the study within the time limitations previously set, the office interviews could not be completed on more than 51 families. In the beginning of the study, some difficulty was experienced in arranging office interviews, and it was thought that the second interview might have to take place in the home. This did not prove to be so except for three families. The children in families who had the second interview in the home were not tested.

A breakdown of the sample according to data obtained for both family units and children is seen in Table 1.

In only three of the families who refused to participate was the reason for refusal an unwillingness on the part of the parents to involve themselves in further discussion about adoption. The interviewer surmised that these families had not shared the fact of adoption with the children. In most cases of refusal the families were busy with work schedules or obviously had no interest in research and did not want to be bothered. Both husband and wife frequently worked in these black families. There were slightly more refusals in the traditional adoption group, the group that had completed legal adoption and therefore had no further contact with the agency. In the quasi-adoption group many more families were still receiving service from the agency.

This is a highly mobile group of families, with frequent address changes. For this reason it was impossible to locate 18 of the families. No forwarding address was left and

16

TABLE 1

Distribution of 123 Families, by Data Available

Data Available*	Quasi		Traditional		Total	
	Family Units	Chil- dren	Family Units	Chil- dren	Family Units	Chil- dren
Home and office interview children seen	26	28	25	27	51	55
Home and office interview children not seen.	2	2	1	1	3	3
Home interview only	11	13	11	11	22	24
Refusals	8	10	14	15	22	25
Unable to locate	10	10	8	8	18	18
Child deceased	1	1	—	—	1	1
Status changed to foster care. . . .	2	3	—	—	2	3
Did not contact for interview . . .	3	4	1	1	4	5
TOTAL	63	71	60	63	123	134

*Case record and service data available on all categories.

no other means of contacting the family was possible. On both the refusal group and nonlocatable group, data were available from the case record at the time of adoption study. Service data were also recorded. It was possible, therefore, to compare the sample group with this group of families who were not seen. An analysis of these comparative data is found in the chapter on Analysis of Data.

E. Procedure for Data Collection

It was decided to obtain all of the data in two contacts with these families. To assure their cooperation, the demands on their time were kept to a minimum. A visit to the home was the first step in data collection. It was thought that a home interview would better prepare the family for the nature of the study and for next steps.

The family was first contacted by a letter signed by the executive director of the Children's Aid Society of Pennsylvania requesting the family's participation in the study. A followup telephone call was made by the interviewer to set a home appointment time.

1. Home Interview

The home interviews were conducted by two experienced social workers and one experienced sociologist who were engaged specifically for this research project. None of the interviewers was connected with the adoption study or supervision of these families. The interviews, which were taped on portable recorders, were conducted on evenings and weekends. The hour-long tapes were usually sufficient to obtain an interview with both mother and father separately. The families were told that one purpose of the study was to let us know how the adoption families were progressing and, in this way, to help other families who wanted to adopt black children. The families were reassured that the interview data were confidential and would not be shared with anyone at the agency. Since it was believed that most of the families would feel free to discuss the child, the focus of the home interview was on the child and the parents' feelings and attitudes about being parents, and adoptive parents in particular. Interview Schedules I through IV were completed in the home. The interviewer explained that there would be an interview at the agency offices to which the parents and child would be requested to come. Again, the parents were assured that the tasks for the child would be game-like, and would in no way deal with the subject of adoption or the child's past.

2. Office Interview

The office interviews were conducted by two social workers, also experienced and especially selected for this project. They were different interviewers from those who interviewed in the home, and had no access to the home interview data. This arrangement assured that the data collected during the office interview were completely independent of the home interview data. The office interviews were conducted on Saturdays to allow both father and mother to accompany the child to the office. The office interview involved the parents in discussion of their own background and early life, as well as a discussion of factors in their marriage. The interviews were taped. The child was seen simultaneously as the parents were interviewed. Two experienced child psychologists were employed to administer the psychological instruments. There were four observers in all, two for each session. Of these, two were graduate social workers, one was a student psychologist and one an elementary school teacher.

The procedure was as follows: The parents and child were invited to come to the room set up for testing. The interaction situation was presented first, with the parents and child left alone in the testing room while the observers recorded the behavior of both parents and child. This procedure was short, taking about 5 minutes. The child then remained with the psychologist for administration of the Binet intelligence test and the Doll Play. Each parent was interviewed individually by the interviewer, and data were obtained for Schedules V, VI and VII. Following the testing session with the child, the parents had an opportunity to talk with the psychologist about his or her findings, and also to ask any questions about the child that concerned them. The office interview lasted about an hour and a half.

The distribution of the home and office interviews by sex and race of the interviewer or psychologist can be seen in Tables 2, 3 and 4.

TABLE 2

Home Interviews, by Sex and Race of Interviewer

Sex and Race of Interviewer	Quasi	Traditional	Total
Black female	15	12	27
White male	14	14	28
Black male	10	11	21
Total	39	37	76

TABLE 3

Office Interviews, by Sex and Race of Interviewer

Sex and Race of Interviewer	Quasi	Traditional	Total
Asian female	15	13	28
White female	13	13	26
Total	28	26	54

TABLE 4

Children Tested, by Sex and Race of Psychologist

Sex and Race of Psychologist	Quasi	Traditional	Total
White female	12	17	29
Black male	17	9	26
Total	29	26	55

3. Case Record Data and Service Data

As the home and office interviews were proceeding, separate raters for these two areas of data were at work filling out the respective schedules. These raters were also experienced social workers but not involved in any way with the adoption procedures at the agency.

Following the completion of the data collection, a letter was sent to each family thanking them for their participation in the study.

References

1. Robin K. Banks and Daniel Cappon, "Developmental Deprivation and Mental Illness: A Study of 20 Questions," *Child Development,* XXXIV (1963), 709-718.

2. Rachel Dunaway Cox, *Youth into Maturity* (New York: Mental Health Materials Center, 1970).

3. Erik Erikson, *Childhood and Society* (New York: W. W. Norton, 1950).

4. "The Pursuit of Promise: The Intellectually Superior Child in a Deprived Social Area" (New York: Community Service Society of New York, 1967, mimeographed).

5. A. Thomas *et al., Temperament and Behavior Disorders in Children* (New York: New York University Press, 1968).

6. Gordon Hamilton, *Theory and Practice of Social Casework* (New York: Columbia University Press, 1951), 241-270.

7. *Ibid.,* 249.

8. David Lynn, *Structured Doll Play Test,* (Denver: Test Developments, 1959).

9. Robert R. Sears, Eleanor Maccoby and Harry Levin, *The Patterns of Child Rearing* (Evanston, Ill.: Row Peterson, 1957).

10. Barbara A. Merrill, "A Measurement of Mother-Child Interaction," *Journal of Abnormal and Social Psychology,* V. 41 (1946), 37-49.

11. Bernard Rosen and Ray D'Andrade, "The Psychosocial Origins of Achievement Motivation," *Sociometry, XXII* (1959), 185-217.

12. Michael Zunich, "Children's Reactions to Failure," *Journal of Genetic Psychology,* CIV, No. 1 (1964), 19-24.

13. Marion J. Winterbottom, "The Relation of Childhood Training in Independence to Achievement Motivation," referred to by Irvin Child in "Socialization," in Gardner Lindzey, ed., *Handbook of Social Psychology, Vol. 2* (Cambridge, Mass.: Addison-Wesley, 1954).

3

Analysis of Data

COMPARISON OF THE INTERVIEW AND NONINTERVIEW GROUPS

The process of obtaining the samples of quasi-adoption and traditional adoption cases was discussed in the chapter on methodology. The final Ns of the two samples were 43 quasi- and 39 traditional adopted children. All references to cases in the following analysis refer to children. These 82 children were in families who had at least a followup home interview, if not an office interview. It was important to know how well these cases represented the total quasi and traditional populations. To check on this and on possible biases arising from the refusal or inaccessibility of certain families, the non-interview cases were compared with the interview cases on a number of variables derived from agency case record data.

The 28 nonsample (noninterview) quasi cases were compared with the 43 sample quasi cases, and the 24 nonsample traditional cases were compared with the 39 sample traditional cases on 34 variables representing demographic, parent, family, and child background factors. In order to pick up more readily any differences between the sample and nonsample groups, the .20 level of significance was selected. The Chi-Square Two-Sample Test was applied to these data.

There were only two variables on which differences were found between the traditional adoption sample and nonsample groups. One of these was the child's age at placement. There were proportionally more sample children than nonsample in the youngest age range at the time of placement, as shown in Table 5.

Since adoptive couples generally prefer the children to be as young as possible at the time of placement, it might be possible to interpret this finding to mean that there could have been some dissatisfaction in the nonsample group over not receiving younger children. This would assume that some of the nonsample parents resisted or avoided

TABLE 5

Children's Age at Placement in Traditional Adoption Homes,
by Sample and Nonsample Groups

Age at Placement	Sample		Nonsample	
	Number	Percent	Number	Percent
6 months or less	21	54	7	29
7 through 17 months	11	28	14	58
18 months or more	7	18	3	13
Total	39	100	24	100

$X^2 = 4.99$, 2df, p < .10

being interviewed because of such dissatisfaction. Although this is a possibility, it is perhaps more likely that this was a random statistical finding at the relatively conservative .10 level.

The other difference that occurred in comparing the sample and nonsample traditional adoption groups was in the preplacement assessment of the attention span of the children. Table 6 shows these data.

TABLE 6

Attention Span of Children in Traditional Adoption Homes,
by Sample and Nonsample Groups

Attention Span	Sample		Nonsample	
	Number	Percent	Number	Percent
Fleeting attention span	—	—	—	—
Moderate attention span	16	41	5	21
Normal attention span	23	59	19	79
Total	39	100	24	100

$X^2 = 2.72$, 1df, p < .10

Table 6 indicates that proportionally more of the nonsample children were assessed as having a "normal" attention span. This would tend to favor the children of non-interviewed parents, which would presumably rule out any possibility of dissatisfaction among the nonsample group on this factor. Since there were only two areas of significant difference out of 34 possible areas between the traditional adoption sample and nonsample groups, there appears to be no reason to assume that there is a systematic bias in the traditional adoption sample.

The same cannot be said, however, about the quasi-adoption sample. There were six variables on which significant differences were found in comparing the quasi sample and the nonsample groups. Although this number of differences could have occurred by statistical chance, five of the six differences had to do with child background factors, which might suggest some possible systematic or selective process at work.

The attention span variable that was noted in reference to the traditional-adoption sample also reflected a difference between the quasi sample and nonsample groups. In this instance, however, there were significantly (X^2=4.20,1df, p < .05) more children in the sample group within the "normal" category than the nonsample group (60% and 32% respectively). Thus, the sample group is more favorable on this variable.

Another positive trend in favor of the quasi sample group was in respect to the child's length of stay in a shelter or institution prior to placement in the adoptive home. Table 7 shows that somewhat more of the nonsample group spent more than a month in an institution or shelter.

TABLE 7

Length of Quasi Children's Stay in Institution or Shelter,
by Sample and Nonsample Groups

Length of Stay	Sample		Nonsample	
	Number	Percent	Number	Percent
Longer than one month.	7	16	11	39
One month or less	36	84	17	61
Total	43	100	28	100

X^2 = 3.60,1df, p < .10

A third area in which the sample quasi children had more favorable backgrounds was in the feeling tone from the foster mother toward the child during the period prior to adoption placement. As indicated in Table 8, proportionally more of the sample children had foster mothers who displayed positive, warm and accepting feelings toward them.

TABLE 8

Feeling Tone from Foster Mothers Toward Quasi Children,
by Sample and Nonsample Groups

Feeling Tone	Sample		Nonsample	
	Number	Percent	Number	Percent
Negative—rejecting, unwanted	—	—	2	7
Neutral—"a job".	3	7	6	21
Positive—warm, accepting	38	88	13	46
*Never in foster care	—	—	6	21
*No information.	2	5	1	4
Total	43	100	28	99

X^2 = 7.02,1df, p < .01

*Not included in computation of chi-square value.

Another factor on which the quasi sample children were different from the non-sample children was in assessment of their preplacement developmental level. Table 9 shows the distribution of the two groups on this variable.

TABLE 9

Quasi Children's Preplacement Developmental Level,
by Sample and Nonsample Groups

Developmental Level	Sample		Nonsample	
	Number	Percent	Number	Percent
Slow	1	2	—	—
Low-average	11	26	5	18
Average	16	37	19	68
High-average	7	16	1	4
Bright	8	19	3	11
Total	43	100	28	101

$X^2 = 6.64$, 2df, $p < .05$

It is difficult to know whether this distribution is more favorable toward the sample or the nonsample group, or toward neither, because there were more sample children in the low and high ranges, with more nonsample children in the average range. The quasi sample shows proportionally more children in the upper and lower ranges on this variable than the total quasi population. It should be noted that the range of scores in the nonsample group was probably restricted by the number of children who were tested at 6 months or less (see Table 10).

The fifth child variable on which there was a difference between the sample and non-sample quasi children was age at placement. Table 10 indicates that there were more sample children in the oldest age category.

This age distribution tends to reflect more favorably on the nonsample than the

TABLE 10

Age of Quasi Children at Time of Placement,
by Sample and Nonsample Groups

Age	Sample		Nonsample	
	Number	Percent	Number	Percent
6 months or less	8	19	12	43
7 through 17 months	18	42	12	43
18 months or more	17	40	4	14
Total	43	101	28	100

$X^2 = 8.21$, 2df, $p < .05$

sample group, since again the general preference of adoptive parents is to obtain children at the youngest possible age.

The only nonchild variable on which a difference was found between the sample and the nonsample quasi groups was in the husband's current occupation. There were more nonsample husbands (32%) than sample husbands (10%) in the lowest occupational category of "unskilled employe." However, this was barely significant at the .20 level.

On the basis of the foregoing comparisons of the sample and nonsample groups, the traditional adoption sample appears to be representative of the traditional adoption population as defined in this study. The quasi sample appears to be representative on parental and family variables. There were five child variables, however, on which the quasi sample group was not representative of the population, though the differences were not consistently in one direction. For this reason, certain qualifications will have to be kept in mind in interpreting findings related to child variables, particularly those on which the quasi sample was found to be different from the rest (nonsample) of the quasi population.

COMPARISON OF THE QUASI- AND TRADITIONAL ADOPTION SAMPLES ON PREPLACEMENT PARENT AND FAMILY VARIABLES

This section of the analysis is intended to provide a comparative description of the samples representing the two adoption programs under study on variables measuring preplacement data on the family situation and the prospective adoptive parents. In terms of the design of the study outlined schematically in the chapter on Methodology, these preplacement parental-family factors are the independent variables of the study. Although the child factors and service input can affect the outcome variables related to postplacement parent/child functioning, it is to differences between the quasi and traditional samples on the independent variables that we look to account for differences between the two groups on the outcome variables.

In addition to the explanatory function of these independent variables in the analytic scheme of the study, they also served to describe the characteristics and backgrounds of the parents in the two adoption methods, that is to the extent that they were representative of the quasi and traditional populations. As indicated in the previous comparison of sample and nonsample groups, the two samples appeared to be representative on preplacement parental variables.

Since differences between these two samples on the independent variables might explain differences in adoption outcome between the two methods, tests for statistical differences are applied to the distributions described in this section. The Chi-Square Two-Sample Test again is applied to most of the data, and the Komolgorov Smirnov Two-Sample Test is applied to some of the remaining ordinal and interval-level data. In line with the exploratory nature of this study, the .10 level of significance was selected, in contrast to the .05 level, for describing differences as statistically significant in the rest of this analysis.

It should be noted that frequencies representing "insufficient information" categories are not included in the following tables, so the Ns are not always 43 and 39, respectively, for the quasi and traditional samples. When cases are lacking for reasons other than insufficient information, those reasons are footnoted. Except for the "insufficient information" categories, the full range of categories or intervals is reported on each distribution, even though it was often necessary to collapse categories to meet the requirements of the chi-square test, as indicated by the reported degrees of freedom.

Among the salient preplacement factors on which the two samples were compared was the age of the parents at application. As Table 11 shows, the quasi mothers were older as a group than the traditional adoption mothers. The quasi mothers had a mean age of 39.2 years; mothers under the traditional adoption method had a mean age of 35.0.

The same trend was clearly evident in Table 12 among the fathers, even though the difference between the quasi- and traditional adoption fathers just missed being statistical-

TABLE 11

Mother's Age at Application, by Adoption Method

Age	Quasi		Traditional	
	Number	Percent	Number	Percent
21-25 years	—	—	3	8
26-30 years	3	7	6	16
31-35 years	9	21	11	29
36-40 years	13	31	11	29
41-45 years	11	26	3	8
46-50 years	4	10	4	10
51-55 years	2	5	—	—
Total	42	100	38	100

*K_D=.241, p < .10

TABLE 12

Father's Age at Application, by Adoption Method

Age	Quasi		Traditional	
	Number	Percent	Number	Percent
21-25 years	—	—	1	3
26-30 years	1	2	6	15
31-35 years	11	26	8	21
36-40 years	7	16	11	28
41-45 years	12	28	6	15
46-50 years	9	21	6	15
51-55 years	2	5	1	3
56 and over	1	2	—	—
Total	43	100	39	100

NS, p > .10

---

*Komolgorov-Smirnov Differences (K_D) are reported as proportions, rather than as percentages, to three decimal places throughout the analysis.

ly significant. The mean age of the fathers under the quasi method was 41.2; the traditional-method fathers had a mean age of 37.6.

In line with the generally older age range of the quasi mothers and fathers, it was also found that the quasi parents had been married longer. The mean length of marriage at application was 10.8 years for quasi parents and 8.5 years for parents in the traditional adoption sample.

Another variable on which there was a significant difference between the two adoption methods was in the number of natural children the couples had by their current marriage. The quasi parents had more children than the traditionals. The difference was most marked when comparing the two groups in terms of the proportion of couples having no children at all. Table 13 shows this difference.

TABLE 13

Number of Children of Current Marriage, by Adoption Method

Number of Children	Quasi		Traditional	
	Number	Percent	Number	Percent
None	21	49	30	77
One	12	28	5	13
Two	6	14	3	8
Three	2	5	1	3
Four	2	5	—	—
Total	43	101	39	101

$K_D = .281$, $p < .05$

The higher incidence of childlessness among the traditional adoption couples was probably a function of the greater occurrence of infertility of the parents in that program. Significantly more fertility studies were made of the traditional-adoption fathers (46% to 14%, $X^2 = 9.85$, 1df, $p < .01$) and of the traditional adoption mothers (57% to 26%, $X^2 = 8.05$, 1df, $p < .01$). In addition to the fertility factor, the generally larger number of children in quasi homes could also be reflective of the adding of a new pool of fertile adoptive parents who were willing to adopt children and add them to their families of natural children with the introduction of the financial support feature of the quasi-adoption program.

A finding that is probably related to the fertility factor and to the difference in ages between the two groups of parents was the expressed age preference for the adoptive child. The couples under the traditional method expressed a significantly greater preference for children under 2 years of age, probably indicative of the greater need of and motivation for infants in this less fertile group.

Because of the scarcity of cases in the categories of "No preference" and "Mixed," the chi-square test was applied only to the two categories of "under 2" and "2 years and over." As can be seen from Table 14, 94% of the couples in the traditional adoption program wanted children under 2 years of age. Conversely, just over half, or 58%, of the quasi couples preferred the younger children.

TABLE 14

Couple's Indicated Preference for Age of Child,
by Adoption Method

	Quasi		Traditional	
Age Preference	Number	Percent	Number	Percent
No preference	1	3	—	—
Under 2 years	22	58	33	94
2 years and over	14	37	2	6
Mixed (mother indicated under 2 years, father 2 years and over)	1	3	—	—
Total	38	101	35	100

$X^2 = 11.88$, 1df, p $<$ .001

In a comparison of the two samples on the socioeconomic variables of husband's occupation, income, education and social class position, the quasi group showed a consistently lower or more marginal ranking than the traditional families.

The differences between the quasi and traditional samples were close to but not quite statistically significant on each of these socioeconomic variables. It should be noted here that the earlier comparison of sample and nonsample groups showed that a disproportionate number of quasi fathers in the lowest occupational rung were not in the sample group. It is possible that the difference between the quasi and traditional groups would have been statistically significant if the quasi sample had been more representative of the quasi population on this variable. This finding is, of course, consistent with the expectations and intent of the agency that a number of the quasi families would need financial

TABLE 15

Husband's Current Occupation, by Adoption Method

	Quasi		Traditional	
Occupation	Number	Percent	Number	Percent
Executive, professional, etc.	—	—	2	5
Business mgr., lesser professional, etc.	1	2	2	5
Administrator, semiprofessional, etc.	1	2	6	15
Clerical, sales, small businessman, etc.	8	19	8	21
Skilled manual employe, etc.	16	37	9	23
Semiskilled worker, etc.	13	30	8	21
Unskilled worker, etc..	4	9	4	10
Total	43	99	39	100

NS, p $>$ .10

support to enable them to take on the responsibility of adopting a child, because of their more marginal economic circumstances.

The data on husband's occupation at the time of application are presented in Table 15.

It can be seen from Table 15 that there was a rather even distribution of traditional adoption husbands throughout the occupational ladder. The bulk of the quasi husbands (76%) on the other hand, were found in the three lowest occupational rungs. There would have been a larger percentage of quasi husbands in the lowest category of "unskilled worker" if the sample had been in line with the actual quasi population on this dimension.

The same trend as in occupation is evident in comparing the income distributions of the two groups in Table 16.

TABLE 16

Father's Current Weekly Income, by Adoption Method

Weekly Income	Quasi		Traditional	
	Number	Percent	Number	Percent
75-99 dollars	5	13	1	3
100-149 dollars	17	43	10	29
150-199 dollars	12	30	16	46
200-249 dollars	4	10	6	17
250-299 dollars	1	2	1	3
300 or more dollars	1	2	1	3
Total , , , , , , , , , , , , , , , , ,	40	100	35	101

NS, p > .10

Over half (56%) of the group of quasi fathers were making under $150 a week, as compared with one-third (32%) of the traditional adoption fathers.

TABLE 17

Husband's Education, by Adoption Method

Education	Quasi		Traditional	
	Number	Percent	Number	Percent
Graduate or professional training . .	1	2	1	3
College graduate	—	—	5	13
Partial college training	3	7	6	15
High school graduate	16	39	14	36
Partial high school	10	24	6	15
7th to 9th grade	11	27	6	15
Under 7th grade	—	—	1	3
Total	41	99	39	100

NS, p > .10

Table 17 demonstrates the same tendencies as far as husband's education is concerned.

The difference between the two groups is indicated by the fact that 31% of the traditional adoption husbands had some training beyond high school, as compared with only 9% of the quasi husbands.

When the occupations and education of the husbands were combined into the Hollingshead Two-Factor Index of Social Class Position, the following distributions were obtained:

TABLE 18

Husband's Social Class Position, by Adoption Method

Class Position	Quasi		Traditional	
	Number	Percent	Number	Percent
I (upper)	—	—	1	3
II	1	2	3	8
III	3	7	7	18
IV	21	51	16	41
V (lower)	16	39	12	31
Total	41	99	39	101

NS, p > .10

Again, although not quite statistically significant, there was a trend toward lower social class position for the quasi husbands. Only 9% of them were classified in the three upper positions, as compared with 29% of the traditional-adoption husbands.

Although the quasi fathers had somewhat less education, income and occupational status than the traditional adoption fathers, it was of considerable interest to note that the traditional adoption fathers had more evidence of deprivation in their backgrounds. The overall score of deprivation, which consists of a cumulative count of potentially negative early life experience items, is indicated for the quasi- and traditional adoption fathers in Table 19.

TABLE 19

Deprivation Score in Father's Background, by Adoption Method

Deprivation Score	Quasi		Traditional	
	Number	Percent	Number	Percent
0-1 negative items	12	86	6	38
2-3 negative items	—	—	5	31
4 or more negative items	2	14	5	31
Total	14	100	16	100

$X^2 = 7.32$, 1df, p < .01

The chi-square value in Table 19 was computed by breaking the distribution into a dichotomous arrangement of "0-1 negative items" and combining the two categories of "2-3" and "4 or more." Since sufficient data were available for less than half of the quasi sample and just a bit more than half of the traditional sample, this statistically significant finding on father's deprivation might not hold for the total samples.

Another background variable on the fathers that showed a significant difference was the item indicating whether both parents of the father were in the home when he was a child. Again, there were insufficient data on over half of the quasi sample and almost half of the traditional. However, as Table 20 shows, significantly more of the quasi fathers on whom there were data came from intact families as children.

TABLE 20

Father's Family Background, by Adoption Method

Family Structure	Quasi		Traditional	
	Number	Percent	Number	Percent
Both parents in the home	12	86	7	44
Mother only in the home	—	—	4	25
Father only in the home	—	—	2	12
Neither parent in the home	2	14	3	19
Total	14	100	16	100

$X^2 = 5.62$, 1df, $p < .05$

It is of interest to note the rating of deprivation in the mothers' backgrounds, in the light of the finding on the fathers. Table 21 gives the breakdown for the mothers.

The quasi and traditional mothers looked very similar in terms of possible deprivation in their backgrounds. They were also quite similar in other background factors such as the size of their families, number of siblings, and whether both parents were in the home. If there is a difference in the later parental functioning of the quasi- and traditional adoption mothers it could not be based on any difference in early life experience in terms of the data available.

TABLE 21

Deprivation Score in Mother's Background, by Adoption Method

Deprivation Score	Quasi		Traditional	
	Number	Percent	Number	Percent
0-1 negative items	17	65	16	57
2-3 negative items	3	12	7	25
4 or more negative items	6	23	5	18
Total	26	100	28	100

NS, $p > .10$

One general area in which there were significant differences between the quasi and traditional families was in housing and housekeeping standards. The traditional adoption families had residences that were in a better state of repair than the quasi families.

TABLE 22

State of Repair of Family Residence, by Adoption Method

| | Quasi | | Traditional | |
State of Repair	Number	Percent	Number	Percent
Poor to fair	22	51	8	20
Good	21	49	31	80
Total	43	100	39	100

$X^2 = 8.28$, 1df, p < .01

About half of the quasi residences were in the "Poor to fair" range, compared with only one-fifth of the traditional adoption homes. This situation could be due to substandard housing in the quasi sample, which the families themselves could not repair. However, there was a marked difference in the cleanliness of the residence by type of adoption family. Table 23 shows this difference.

TABLE 23

Cleanliness of Residence, by Adoption Method

| | Quasi | | Traditional | |
Cleanliness	Number	Percent	Number	Percent
Dirty	1	2	—	—
Moderately clean	30	70	15	38
Spotless	12	28	24	62
Total	43	100	39	100

$X^2 = 9.39$, 1df, p < .01

In summary, the comparative descriptions of the families in the two adoption programs show that the quasi families tended to have somewhat lower socioeconomic and financial situations, though the differences did not reach statistical significance given the size of the samples. There was no more evidence of deprivation in the backgrounds of the quasi parents. In fact, based on a relatively small number of cases, it was possible that the traditional adoption fathers might have had more deprivation in their backgrounds. The mothers in the two adoption methods seemed similar in background, but the residences of the quasi families were significantly poorer in state of repair and cleanliness.

COMPARISON OF THE SAMPLES ON INTERVENING
FACTORS: CHILDREN AND SERVICE

A. Children

In the general scheme for analysis of data, the child placed was conceived of as an intervening factor in the sense that child characteristics and functioning could have an effect on parental functioning and satisfaction, and overall family functioning. If the children placed in the two types of adoptive homes are similar in background and functioning at the time of placement, later differences in adoption outcome (dependent variables) between the two methods would not be explained on the basis of child factors. This section of the analysis is devoted to a comparison of the quasi- and traditional adoption children on preplacement factors.

One characteristic of central importance in any such comparison is that of sex. Proportionally, how many boys and girls were placed in each of the two types of adoptive homes? Table 24 gives this breakdown.

TABLE 24

Sex of Child, by Adoption Method

	Quasi		Traditional	
Child's Sex	Number	Percent	Number	Percent
Male	23	54	17	44
Female	20	46	22	56
Total	43	100	39	100

NS, p > .10

Although there is a somewhat larger proportion of boys than girls in the quasi sample, and proportionally more girls than boys in the traditional sample, the difference is not statistically significant.

TABLE 25

Age of Child at Placement, by Adoption Method

	Quasi		Traditional	
Age at Placement	Number	Percent	Number	Percent
6 months or less	8	19	21	54
7 through 17 months	18	42	11	28
18 months or more	17	39	7	18
Total	43	100	39	100

$X^2 = 10.68$, 2df, p < .01

TABLE 26

Children's Preplacement Developmental Level, by Adoption Method

Developmental Level	Quasi		Traditional	
	Number	Percent	Number	Percent
Slow	1	2	—	—
Low-average	11	26	2	5
Average	16	37	29	74
High-average	7	16	5	13
Bright	8	19	3	8
Total	43	100	39	100

$X^2 = 10.30$, 2df, $p < .01$

Another variable of considerable importance is the age of the child at the time of place-ment in the adoptive home. In this variable there is a significant difference between the quasi and traditional samples, as illustrated in Table 25.

Table 25 indicates that the children in the traditional adoption sample were younger as a group at the time of placement than were the quasi children. This would appear to be consistent with the somewhat older age of the quasi parents and their greater willingness to take older children, as indicated earlier in the analysis. It should be recalled, however, that neither the quasi- nor the traditional adoption sample was representative of its population on this variable. The quasi sample was significantly older than the nonsample quasi children, and the traditional adoption sample was younger than its respective nonsample group. Both of these facts make the quasi and traditional samples more dis-similar on this variable than their respective populations would be.

A second variable on which there was a significant difference between the quasi and traditional samples was the child's preplacement developmental level. Table 26 indicates that the most notable difference was in the "average" category, where proportionally there were twice as many traditional adoption children.

In addition to the "average" category, there were notably more quasi children in the "low-average" and "low" categories than there were traditional adoption children. Looked at in another way, 95% of the traditional adoption children were average or brighter.

In addition to the foregoing significant differences, there were significantly more negative factors in the backgrounds of the quasi children. This applied to both en-vironmental and constitutional factors in the child's past. As reported in the chapter on methodology, a cumulative scoring system for negative environmental and constitutional factors was derived and applied to case record data. The environmental score included items on early life experiences of the child, such as overt neglect or abuse, and number of foster homes. The distribution of the cumulative scores for the children in the two samples is given in Table 27.

Of course, the higher the scores the more negative the backgrounds, so the quasi children did not fare so well on early environmental factors. As examples of individual factors in these scores, there were more than twice as many quasi-adoption children than traditional adoption children in two or more foster homes prior to adoptive placement.

TABLE 27

Score on Negative Environmental Factors in the Child's
Background, by Adoption Method

	Quasi		Traditional	
Score	Number	Percent	Number	Percent
0-1.	14	33	19	53
2-3	9	21	15	42
4 and over	19	45	2	6
Total	42	99	36	101

$X^2 = 15.65$, 2df, p < .001

There were 10 out of 43 (23%) quasi children in two or more foster homes, as compared with four out of 39 (10%) traditional adoption children. Another factor was length of time in an institution or shelter during infancy. In this instance seven of the quasi children were in institutions or shelters for longer than a month, whereas none of the traditional adoption children was. Further, three quasi children had been exposed to overt neglect or abuse prior to placement, whereas none of the traditional adoption children had been. Individually, the factors are not statistically significant because of the small numbers involved, but the combined or cumulative scores indicate the differences.

The cumulative scores on negative constitutional factors are given in Table 28.

TABLE 28

Score on Negative Constitutional Factors in the
Child's Background, by Adoption Method

	Quasi		Traditional	
Score	Number	Percent	Number	Percent
1-4.	13	33	22	60
5-8.	12	31	9	24
9 and over	14	36	6	16
Total	39	100	37	100

$X^2 = 5.89$, 2df, p < .10

The difference between the quasi- and traditional adoption children on individual constitutional factors showed up in such items as evidence that the birth mother was mentally limited. In five quasi cases the birth mother was felt to be mentally limited, as compared with only one case in the traditional sample. On the attention-span item, three quasi children and no traditional adoption children were found to have fleeting spans. Again, the numbers were small, but the cumulative effect was for a significant difference between the two groups on constitutional factors.

Although the difference was not so great on constitutional factors as it was on environmental background factors, when the two cumulative scores were combined in a sum of negative background scores, the difference between the two groups of children was, of course, even greater. Table 29 illustrates this.

TABLE 29

Sum of Negative Scores on Environmental and
Constitutional Factors in the Child's Background

Sum of Scores	Quasi		Traditional	
	Number	Percent	Number	Percent
1-7	13	31	28	74
8-13	19	45	9	24
14-24	10	24	1	3
Total	42	100	38	101

$X^2 = 16.26$, df = 2, p < .001

The foregoing findings of more negative background factors in the quasi children should be taken into account in any further analysis of findings. These factors could have a subsequent negative effect on some of the quasi children's later functioning, which could in turn affect parental and overall family functioning. The comparative analysis of postplacement functioning of the children under the two adoption methods should shed light on this matter. In the meantime, there is the other intervening factor of service to consider in the general scheme for analysis.

B. Service

As described in the chapter on methodology, the service input was classified by *types* and by *methods.* The types refer to service categories such as family functioning, financial functioning, etc. The methods refer to approaches the caseworkers take in providing the service. "Administration of a practical service," according to Gordon Hamilton, is the method that includes any activity that assists the client or family to choose or use a social resource. Since "social resource" can mean the agency's own resources, it is to be expected that the quasi families should receive more services of this type. Just on the basis of payments for boarding costs, clothing grants, etc., the frequency of practical services should be greater in the quasi sample. This was indeed the case, as illustrated in Table 30.

The two other service methods in the classification scheme were "supportive treatment." The latter category, which involves a series of interviews in which the worker makes conscious use of relationship to bring about behavioral or attitudinal change, simply did not apply to the casework process reflected in the cases of this study.

The "supportive treatment" service method did occur in the study cases, but there was no significant difference between the quasi- and the traditional adoption cases in the frequency of such services. The reason for this probably lay in the nature of this service method. It is an approach in which the caseworker provides for the client reassurance,

TABLE 30

Frequency of Administration of Practical Services, by Adoption Method

Frequency	Quasi		Traditional	
	Number	Percent	Number	Percent
None	1	2	16	41
One	13	31	19	49
Two	19	45	3	8
Three	5	12	1	3
Four	2	5	—	—
Five or more	2	5	—	—
Total	42	100	39	101

$K_D = .563$, p < .001

encouragement, and the opportunity for ventilation. The worker also uses techniques on an educational level involving suggestion and advice. It can be seen that this approach would apply equally to traditional adoption practice and quasi practice. Table 31 shows the similarity in frequency of supportive treatment services in the two groups.

TABLE 31

Frequency of Supportive Treatment Services, by Adoption Method

Frequency	Quasi		Traditional	
	Number	Percent	Number	Percent
One	13	31	14	36
Two	12	29	13	33
Three	9	21	6	15
Four	6	14	5	13
Five or more	2	5	1	3
Total	42	100	39	100

NS, p > .10

Turning to the service types, as distinct from service methods, the financial assistance services show the most dramatic difference in frequency between the two adoption methods. Table 32 shows this difference.

This difference was to be expected by virtue of the nature of the quasi program. It is particularly in the financial area that the program is geared to enable families to adopt the children who need homes. When it comes to the other types of services, it had been anticipated that the quasi families would receive more. This did not occur, however. The frequency of service in family functioning, physical functioning, social and community functioning, home maintenance, vocational functioning and educational services was remarkably similar.

TABLE 32
Frequency of Financial Assistance Services, by Adoption Method

Frequency	Quasi		Traditional	
	Number	Percent	Number	Percent
None	1	2	37	95
One	41	98	2	5
Total	42	100	39	100

$X^2 = 69.39$, 1df, $p < .0001$

One possible explanation for this finding of similarity is that all the types of services other than financial are provided via the supportive treatment method, as it was defined in this study. Since this service approach is basic to all adoption practice, it was being provided equally to the quasi- and traditional adoption families in all but the financial assistance. On the basis of these findings, then, we can say that the basic service input in the quasi program was the administration of practical services in the form of financial assistance.

One additional point should be made about the service input findings. The prestudy expectation that the quasi families would seek more help in strengthening family life and in making decisions to improve their opportunities apparently was not borne out. The quasi and traditional adoption families received help in these areas in similar amounts, as far as can be gathered from case record data. For this reason, we cannot view the intervening factor of service as a compensating factor in areas such as family and parental functioning when we analyze postplacement functioning and outcome. It may well be that financial assistance can have a "radiating" effect in that it provides an emotional or psychological support indirectly to areas of functioning other than the financial. However, this is next to impossible to determine, so the analysis of the effect of the intervening factor of service has to be restricted to the area of financial functioning.

COMPARISON OF THE SAMPLES OF POSTPLACEMENT FUNCTIONING AND THE OUTCOME VARIABLES

This section of the analysis is directed toward determining the comparative postplacement functioning of the quasi-adoption children and parents versus the traditional adoption children and parents. The parents' postplacement functioning is first viewed in component parts or areas of functioning (parental, marital, etc.) and finally in an overall measure of combining mother and father scores in several areas of functioning which is a dependent or *outcome* variable, according to the conceptual scheme outlined in Chapter 2.

The children's postplacement functioning also is viewed in component parts or areas of functioning based on ratings derived from interviews with the parents and direct observation by the psychologists. There are two overall measures of child functioning, one based on parental report and the other based upon problems observed by the psychologists. These two measures are the dependent variables describing adoption outcome in terms of "child adjustment," as illustrated in the conceptual scheme.

The comparative description of postplacement functioning begins with an analysis of the individual areas or aspects of the mothers' functioning. There were five areas in which the mother's parental functioning was assessed: satisfaction in parental role, acceptance of adoptive role, communication regarding the fact of adoption, parental warmth and affection, and compatibility in parental decision making regarding child-rearing practices. Of these five areas, only one showed a significant (.10 level) difference in the functioning of the quasi- and traditional adoption mothers. That area was "satisfaction in parental role"; the distribution of the two samples on this variable is presented in Table 33.

TABLE 33

Mother's Satisfaction in Parental Role, by Adoption Method

Satisfaction Rating	Quasi		Traditional	
	Number	Percent	Number	Percent
1. Relatively low degree	1	2	—	—
2. Low-average	—	—	—	—
3. Average	1	2	—	—
4. High-average	8	19	3	8
5. High degree	33	77	36	92
Total	43	100	39	100

$X^2 = 3.02$, 1df, $p < .10$

A number of points need to be made about Table 33, since it reflects some features that run throughout the parental-functioning variables. First, the most striking feature was the exceptionally high ratings given the mothers in both adoption methods. Seventy-seven percent of the quasi mothers and 92% of the traditional adoption mothers were given the highest rating by the interviewers. This is obviously far from a normal statistical distribution, even on so few gross intervals or categories. Since the independent judges who listened to the tapes gave ratings that corresponded closely with the interviewers', there had to be some consistent reason or reasons for these high scores.

The primary reason appears to be in the nature of the ratings, which are based essentially on the self-reports of the parents, who tended to give consistently positive reports. The interviewer or judge would have to find some inconsistency or indirect negative indicators in the context of one interview in order to give lower ratings on functioning. A second reason is what might be called the "honeymoon factor," which has to do with the fact that the children in this study were very young preschoolers for the most part. The parents and children were thus in that early stage of relationship that does not have the added dimensions and stresses of school, peer and community adjustment.

In analyzing these ratings, it is evident that they form basically a dichotomy of upper and lower categories of functioning. The bulk of the cases fall in the upper category, which is always the highest or fifth rank in the five-category scales, as represented in Table 33. Although only a minority of both quasi- and traditional adoption cases fall in the lower functioning category, it is a rather consistent minority that is numerically large enough to reflect a pattern in the functioning of the mothers and fathers.

As mentioned earlier, none of the other four areas of parental functioning showed a significant difference between the quasi- and traditional adoption mothers. The area of "acceptance of adoptive role" showed 69% of the quasi mothers and 79% of the traditional mothers in the upper category of functioning. In "communication of the fact of adoption," 56% of the quasi mothers and 67% of the traditional mothers were in the upper category. On "parental warmth and affection," 81% of the quasi mothers were in the upper category, as compared with 90% of the traditional mothers. Finally, there were 59% of the quasi mothers in the upper category of "compatibility in parental decision making," as compared with 69% of the traditional mothers. Thus, the trend on all five of these parental functioning variables favored the traditional adoption mothers, though only "satisfaction in parental role" showed a statistically significant difference.

Analysis of data on the fathers on the same five variables of parental functioning shows that there were statistically significant differences between the quasi- and traditional adoption fathers in two areas of functioning — i.e., "acceptance of adoptive role" and "communication regarding the fact of adoption." The distribution on the "acceptance" variable is presented in Table 34.

TABLE 34

Father's Acceptance of Adoptive Role, by Adoption Method

Acceptance Rating	Quasi		Traditional	
	Number	Percent	Number	Percent
1. Relatively low degree	—	—	—	—
2. Low-average	2	5	2	6
3. Average	5	14	—	—
4. High-average	10	27	7	19
5. High degree	20	54	27	75
Total	37	100	36	100

$X^2 = 3.49$, 1df, $p < .10$

It can be seen that there were not sufficient data on six of the quasi fathers and three of the traditional adoption fathers. However, the Ns are large enough to show the trend and statistical significance of a somewhat lower acceptance of the adoptive role on the part of the quasi fathers. "Acceptance of *adoptive* role" should not be confused with acceptance of *parental* role . Basically, the item has to do with the father's feelings about being an *adoptive* parent, with its differences from the role of natural parent.

The quasi fathers apparently have somewhat less acceptance, though still generally high, than the traditional adoption parents. When this finding is considered in the light of the fathers' rating on communication regarding adoption, there is some consistency in that both the acceptance and communication variables are related specifically to *adoptive* parenting. The other parent items are more general and could apply to natural parents.

At any rate, the quasi fathers showed a significantly lower capacity to communicate about the fact of adoption than the traditional adoption fathers. Table 35 illustrates this.

TABLE 35

Father's Communication Regarding Adoption, by Adoption Method

Communication Capacity	Quasi		Traditional	
	Number	Percent	Number	Percent
1. Relatively low	3	8	4	11
2. Low-average	5	14	3	8
3. Average	7	19	2	6
4. High-average	9	24	6	17
5. High capacity.	13	35	21	58
Total	37	100	36	100

$X^2 = 3.95$, df = 1, p < .05

Although there was greater spread of scores throughout the intervals of the distributions in Table 35, the basic breakdown was still clearly the dichotomous lower and upper, with 35% of the quasi fathers in the upper category, as compared with 58% of the traditional adoption fathers. Thus, the finding on the communication variable was significant, using the chi-square test with one degree of freedom.

The three remaining parental variables on the fathers showed no significant differences between the two samples. On "satisfaction in parental role," 78% of the quasi fathers and 92% of the traditional adoption fathers were in the upper category of satisfaction. On "parental warmth and affection," 78% of the quasi fathers and 89% of the traditional fathers were in the upper category. Thus, the trend was toward somewhat higher functioning on the part of the traditional adoption fathers, but not markedly so or to a statistically significant degree.

There was somewhat of a reversal on the remaining parental variable of "compatibility in parental decision making." Here the trend favored the quasi fathers, who had 69% in the upper category, as compared with 58% of the traditional adoption fathers. This was not a statistically significant difference, as mentioned before, but it was the one difference out of 10 possibilities that favored a quasi- rather than a traditional adoption parent.

Thus, the picture we get from the parental-functioning variables is that the quasi mothers showed a significantly lower satisfaction in their parental roles, and the quasi fathers showed a lower acceptance of the adoptive role and a lower capacity for communication about adoption. The finding concerning the mothers' satisfaction is not easily interpreted. It is possible that the more questionable environmental and constitutional backgrounds in some of the quasi children was showing up in later functioning and taking some toll of the mothers' satisfaction in the maternal role. However, findings based on the parents' (and specifically the mothers') reports on the behavior of the children showed no significant difference between quasi- and traditional adoption children. This could be explained by the generally positive reports on the children made by the mothers, which would tend to blur differences and any possible statistical relationship between child behavior and maternal satisfaction. On the other hand, the findings on the fathers are not so difficult to interpret. That the significant findings were on acceptance of the *adoptive role* and communication about the *fact of adoption* suggests greater ambivalence toward adoption on the part of the quasi fathers.

Given these three significant findings, and the general trend in favor of the traditional adoption parents on most of the parental variables, when the ratings of both parents in all areas of parental functioning were combined into the overall or *outcome measure on parental functioning* there was a significant difference between the quasi- and traditional adoption parents. This is shown in Table 36.

TABLE 36

Combined Rating on Parental Functioning, by Adoption Method

Rating	Quasi		Traditional	
	Number	Percent	Number	Percent
Lower range	9	21	1	3
Middle range	14	33	11	28
Upper range	20	46	27	69
Total	43	100	39	100

$X^2 = 7.47$, 2df, p < .05

The ranges of the ratings in Table 36 were derived by averaging the parental ratings of mother and father into a mean score based on the five-point scale running from "relatively low" (value of 1) to "high degree" (value of 5). The resulting means actually distributed themselves into the three categories given in Table 36. For the most part, parents in the "upper" category had ratings of "high degree" on most of the individual parental items. The parents in the "middle range" were predominantly in the "high-average" categories on individual items, and the "lower range" parents generally were in the "average" to "low-average" categories.

Thus, the findings indicate that there was a significant difference between the quasi parents and the traditional adoption parents on the dependent or outcome variable of parental functioning. What does this finding mean? It means that the parental functioning of the quasi parents was somewhat lower than the traditional adoption parents, but it does not mean that the functioning of the quasi parents was poor. In critical areas such as parental warmth and affection, the difference in the two adoption methods was not statistically significant. The ratings of the parents in both methods are rather high, though undoubtedly inflated by the self-report factor. Additional meaning can be attached to this finding when we look at it in relation to the other outcome measures of the child's postplacement adjustment.

Assessment of the children's postplacement adjustment was based on two sources of data: the parents' perceptions of the child's behavior along certain dimensions, and the psychologist's direct observations in the test situation. The parents' perceptions of the child's adjustment were obtained during the home interview phase of the followup. The testing and observation by the psychologist occurred at the later office interview. It should be recalled from the earlier description of the data collection process that 43 quasi- and 39 traditional adoption children were included in the home interview phase, whereas only 28 quasi- and 27 traditional adoption children were seen in the office followup.

The scales for rating the children's behavior according to parental perceptions are given in Schedule III in the Appendix. Conceptually, the scales are bipolar in nature, with extremes of behavior at opposite ends of a continuum and the best balance of behavior in the middle, or position "5." Two subscales running from "1," a poor adjustment rating, to "5," the best adjustment, were used to represent each of the following behavioral continuums: Aggressive/passive; dependent/independent; defiant/compliant; destructive/careful; responsive/withdrawn; greedy/fussy about food; fearful/reckless; jealous/accepting of siblings. No statistically significant differences were found on any of the foregoing 16 subscales or eight combined scales. Finally, all of the items were averaged in a combined (mother and father) parental rating on child functioning. The highest possible scale position on this rating was 5, as in the component scales and subscales, and the lowest position was 1. However, because of the tendency toward inflated, positive parental reports, none of the children in the quasi or traditional sample had a composite score lower than 2.5, or an "average" adjustment rating. For this reason, the combined parental rating on child functioning was compressed into three ordinal categories, as in the earlier "Combined Rating on Parental Functioning": "Lower range" (scale points 2.5 to 4.0), "Middle range" (scale points 4.0 to 4.5), and "Upper range" (4.5 to 5.0). The comparison of quasi- and traditional adoption children by this breakdown is given in Table 37.

TABLE 37

Combined Parents' Rating on Child Functioning, by Adoption Method

Child Functioning	Quasi		Traditional	
	Number	Percent	Number	Percent
Lower range	12	28	10	26
Middle range	16	37	21	54
Upper range	15	35	8	20
Total	43	100	39	100

NS, p > .10

There was no statistically significant difference between the quasi- and traditional adoption children in their behavioral functioning as assessed by the combined parental rating. The slightly higher proportion of quasi children in the upper range is more apparent than real. Not only was it not statistically significant, but the actual scale-point differences between the middle and upper ranges were slight, 4.0 and 4.5 and 4.5 to 5.0, respectively.

The psychologist's ratings of problems in the child at the time of testing in the office provided a measure of postplacement child functioning that was independent of the parents' report or perception. The ratings are actually the *number* of problems reported by the psychologist on the basis of his observations. The comparison of the quasi- and traditional adoption children on this variable is given in Table 38.

TABLE 38

Number of Problems Observed by Psychologist, by Adoption Method

Problems Observed	Quasi		Traditional	
	Number	Percent	Number	Percent
None	11	39	16	59
One	9	32	8	30
Two	4	14	1	4
Three	3	11	—	—
Four	1	4	1	4
Five	—	—	1	4
Total	28	100	27	101

NS, p > .10

Again, there was no significant difference between the quasi- and traditional adoption children, this time by the independent measure of problems by the psychologists. There is a tendency illustrated in Table 38 that suggests more problems in the quasi group. Whether this would have become large enough for statistical significance if all the children in the initial sample had been tested in the office followup is a moot question. It is apparent that the psychologists and the adoptive parents were somewhat at variance in rating the children. The combined parental ratings favor the quasi children slightly while the psychologists' observations favor the traditional adoption children somewhat.

The salient point of the foregoing analysis is that *neither* outcome measure, psycho-

TABLE 39

Age and Sex of the Children Tested, by Adoption Method

Age	Quasi		Traditional		
	M	F	M	F	Total
3 years	3	1	3	2	9
4 years	4	5	4	7	20
5 years	3	5	3	3	14
6 years	5	2	2	3	12
Total	15	13	12	15	55

logical or parental, showed a statistically significant difference between the quasi- and traditional adoption children in postplacement adjustment.

In addition to outcome ratings by the psychologists and parents, other results are interesting as descriptive of this sample of children. The distribution of age and sex of children tested is seen in Table 39.

There were no significant differences in age and sex factors between the quasi- and traditional adoption children.

As noted previously, both black and white examiners administered the Stanford-Binet Intelligence Test. The IQ results were not significantly different by race of examiner and were, in fact, almost identical (see Table 40). The median IQ obtained by the black examiner was almost identical with that of the white examiner (102 vs. 103.5).

TABLE 40

IQ Results, by Race of the Examiner

Race	IQ < 85	86-100	101-115	116 >	Total
White	3	10	11	5	29
Black	3	9	9	5	26
Total	6	19	20	10	55

The range of IQ scores for the combined groups was from 77 to 133, and the distribution was not deviant from that expected in the general population (see Table 41). It is interesting to note that 18% scored at 116 or above. This seems to contraindicate findings that black children do poorly on verbal tests of intelligence.

Table 41 shows that there is a significant difference in intelligence between the quasi- and traditional adoption groups, with the latter showing the higher scores. One explanation of this finding may be the lower socioeconomic factors in the quasi-adoption homes. A second and more likely explanation may be the fact that the children

TABLE 41

IQ Results, by Adoption Method

IQ	Quasi Number	Percent	Traditional Number	Percent	Total Number	Percent
< 85	4	14	2	7	6	11
86-100	12	43	7	26	19	35
101-115	10	36	10	37	20	36
116 >	2	7	8	30	10	18
Total	28	100	27	100	55	100

$X^2 = 5.35$, 2df, $p > .05 < .10$

placed in quasi-adoption homes, compared with those placed in traditional homes, were somewhat slower-developing infants, with a greater number of potentially limiting constitutional and environmental factors. In other words, they came from more limited backgrounds, had more birth problems and more traumatic early living experiences. One of the goals in developing the quasi-adoption program was to provide homes for just such children. Hence it is not surprising to see them functioning somewhat lower in intelligence at this time. The encouraging finding is that the range of intelligence was normal, with no mentally deficient children. The more important fact is that there were no differences in overall adjustment between the two groups of children.

Data from the Doll Play are contained in Tables 42, 43 and 44.

Few in this sample of young children made mature object choices in all three situations where such choice was given. Most of them selected three immature objects or two out of two immature objects. No significant pattern was discernible by age, though the 3-year-olds rarely made mature choices. The girls tended to make fewer mature choices than the boys, which may say something about the boy child's need to be less a "baby.' No other significant relationships to object choice were observed.

The predominant pattern in choice of parent doll was one of equal choice between mother and father. It is interesting that no girls chose the father doll more than the

TABLE 42

Object Choice in Doll Play, by Adoption Method
and Sex of the Child

	Quasi		Traditional		
Object Choice	M	F	M	F	Total
All mature	2	—	1	1	4
Mature > immature	4	3	4	4	15
Immature > mature	7	2	4	7	20
All immature.	2	8	3	3	16
Total	15	13	12	15	55

TABLE 43

Object Choice in Doll Play, by Age and Adoption Method

	Quasi		Traditional		
Age	Mature	Immature	Mature	Immature	Total
3-3[11]	1	3	1	4	9
4-4[11]	3	6	5	6	20
5-5[11]	3	5	1	5	14
6-6[11]	2	5	3	2	12
Total	9	19	10	17	55

46

TABLE 44

Parent Choice in Doll Play, by Adoption Method and Sex of the Child

Parent Choice	Quasi		Traditional		Total
	M	F	M	F	
Father > mother	4	—	3	—	7
Mother > father	3	2	1	5	11
Father = mother	8	11	8	9	36
No information	—	—	—	1	1
Total	15	13	12	15	55

mother doll. All those who deviated from the predominant pattern chose the mother more frequently than the father. Four boys, on the other hand, chose the mother doll more frequently than the father. However, seven boys selected father in preference to mother. These data do not indicate the presence of mother-dominated homes. It must be remembered that these were intact families with both a mother and father present. The tendency was for most children to select either parent doll equally, and if not that, then to select the appropriate like-sex model. In this ego task, it appears that the children reflected imitative behavior rather than libidinal object choices.

A rating was made of the child's imagined comments from parent dolls when the child doll had misbehaved or acted immaturely. Most of the children perceived the parents as neither all punitive nor all supportive, but a healthy mixture of both. Eight children did perceive the parent dolls as mostly punitive, and four children perceived them as mainly supportive. No significant relationships were obtained between these scores and any other variables.

The patterns of behavior in the interaction situation were not varied enough to be of any significance. Both mothers and fathers exhibited a characteristic passive, nonverbal, positive behavior. The parents were generally interested, as onlookers, generally nonverbal and always positive and supportive. The children likewise responded almost uniformly to the task situation. They worked independently and rarely asked for help, though some did look for approval from their parents. The results are not clear-cut enough to draw conclusions about the demonstration of warmth and affection, probably because the task situation did not elicit it. The home interview data indicated that all parents expressed much warmth and affection when describing their children. Possibly the interested-onlooker approach was enough evidence of their affection. With the passivity of the parents in the situation, one can also not conclude much about independence and achievement. The children displayed considerable autonomy and the parents evidenced little control or direction. Yet they also did not encourage the children much in any verbal or nonverbal fashion. It would be interesting to compare these results with those from a white sample matched for social class and age.

STATISTICALLY NONSIGNIFICANT FINDINGS ON OUTCOME VARIABLES

The major focus of the statistical analysis of data up to this point has been comparison of the quasi- and traditional adoption groups. This is because the primary purpose and design of the study were to assess a new program by comparing it with an already existing and established program. In line with this, the quasi and traditional groups were compared in terms of their distribution on all the variables in the study. Only those variables on which significant differences were found were reported in the foregoing analysis, along with certain statistically nonsignificant findings on outcome variables.

Although it is not feasible or sensible to report on all the variables on which no significant differences were found, there were several variables of interest in their own right. These variables are not so critical as the outcome measures of the study, but they have an intrinsic descriptive value and they were considered important in the conceptual framework described in Chapter 2. This section of the analysis focuses on these several variables.

One such set of variables had to do with marital functioning. The parents were assessed on the following marital scales: "Affectional Aspects of the Relationship," "Sexual Relationship," "Finances," "Communication," and finally, "Marital Organization." These were five-point scales running from "low satisfaction" to "high satisfaction." There were no significant statistical differences between the quasi and traditional groups on any of these five scales. There are, however, general features about the distributions that are worth mentioning.

The scale on "marital organization," which has to do with the structured role relationships of the couples, showed a distribution that generally reflected distributions on the other marital scales. Therefore, some discussion of this distribution is useful for obtaining a general idea of the marital functioning of these couples. The husbands had a tendency to report somewhat higher degrees of satisfaction than the wives. This, however, was not a statistically significant difference, and only about half of the fathers were interviewed in terms of these scales. Consequently, a more complete picture can be obtained by looking at the distribution of the wives.

First, only two of the quasi-adoption and only one of the traditional adoption mothers expressed a low degree of satisfaction (scale points 1 and 2). Seven, or 25% of the quasi mothers expressed "average" satisfaction, as compared with three, or 11%, of the traditional adoption mothers. Nineteen, or 68%, of the quasi wives expressed "high satisfaction" (scale points 4 and 5) while 24, or 86%, of the traditional adoption mothers expressed high satisfaction on marital organization. The somewhat higher degrees of satisfaction of the traditional adoption mothers were not, as was mentioned before, statistically significant. What is more salient is the high rating of both groups of wives. When the two groups are combined, 77% show a high degree of satisfaction, while 18% show an average degree and only 5% show a low degree.

When the combined quasi- and traditional distribution on marital organization is correlated with the combined distribution on parental functioning, there is practically no statistical association at all ($r=.06$). This appears to be consistent with the findings of the prior adoption study, which showed that the level of marital functioning is not in itself indicative of the level of parental functioning.[1] A further explanation of this lack of statistical relationship between marital and parental functioning is that the distribution on both variables is skewed in the direction of high functioning. Because of the resulting sameness or lack of variation, there is no possibility of demonstrating a high statistical relationship.

48

Another set of variables of interest in the analysis were those dealing with parental deprivation. It was thought that there would be a relationship between childhood deprivation of the parents and their later parental functioning, such that more childhood deprivation would lead to poorer parental functioning, in the absence of later compensating experiences or personal relationships.

Data were collected on a number of factors that might be indicative of early deprivation, such as adequacy of food, clothing and housing as a child, length of time lived with parents, lived in an institution, in a foster home, etc. (see Schedule V in Appendix). In addition, an overall score of deprivation was derived from a cumulative count of the negative early life experiences reflected in the individual deprivation items. None of the individual variables taken singly showed significant statistical relationships with the outcome variables or by adoption method. However, it will be recalled from the earlier part of this analysis (see Table 19) that there was a significant difference between the quasi- and traditional adoption fathers on their overall deprivation scores, with the traditional adoption fathers showing greater indication of deprivation. This was, of course, a questionable finding because of the small N involved. Since this finding tended to favor the quasi fathers, and since some measures of later parental functioning tended to favor the traditional adoption fathers, it is not surprising that there was no strong correlation (r= -.02) between early deprivation and later parental functioning as far as the fathers were concerned.

The same situation applied to the mothers on these variables. There was no significant relationship (r=.11) between early deprivation of the mothers and their later parental functioning. It will be recalled that the quasi-adoption and traditional adoption mothers looked similar on their overall deprivation scores (see Table 21).

Again, the factor that may be masking any relationship that might exist between the variables is the uniformly high ratings on parental functioning. Even though there was some variation in the deprivation scores of the parents, there was no concomitant variation in parental functioning scores, so no relationship could be found. In view of this it is not surprising that the measures concerning later compensating experiences and persons showed no significant or discernible relationships to outcome.

The relatively small number of cases having measures on early deprivation, later compensating experiences, and the outcome variable of parental functioning really precludes the possibility of finding statistical relationships between these variables. However, this does not mean, for example, that in individual cases there are not actual histories of early deprivation that were compensated for by later life experiences with persons who had a positive influence so that parental functioning was not impaired. Although the statistical analysis does not provide a discernible pattern of relationships among these variables or factors, the following chapter on family profiles provides more of a picture of such patterns through the description of actual study cases.

In summary, it can be said that in this analysis both the quasi- and the traditional adoption samples showed surprisingly high ratings of family and child functioning. Although in part this may be a function of the inflationary effect of self-reports, the professional and skilled interviewers who obtained the reports saw no evidence of gross distortions with respect to their own observations. There were, however, some differences in parental functioning between the two groups of adoptive parents. The overall or combined parental functioning was significantly higher for the traditional adoption families, as were the specific areas of mother's satisfaction in parental role, father's acceptance of adoptive role, and father's communication regarding adoption. That a number of the quasi-adoption children had problem backgrounds did not seem to affect seriously the overall functioning of the quasi families or the later functioning of the children at followup. The outcome measures of child functioning showed no significant differences between the traditional and quasi-adoption children except in intelligence. One note of caution should, however, be sounded here. Because these children were still young and relatively new to the families, there may have been a "honeymoon factor" operating in which the parents were getting a high degree of satisfaction from their functioning well as parents. As the children get older there could develop problems in parental and child functioning that were not evident at the time of the study. However, this could be determined only by a later study of the same families. But, for the present, the parents and children in both the quasi- and traditional adoption homes seem to be functioning well. On the basis of these findings, it appears that the quasi program is a viable one that is providing permanent homes for black children without negative effects on the well-being of the children involved.

Reference

1. Elizabeth A. Lawder *et al., A Followup Study of Adoptions: Post-Placement Functioning of Adoption Families, Vol. 1* (New York: Child Welfare League of America, 1970), 117.

4

Illustrations of Family Functioning

A. FAMILY FACTORS

General Characteristics and Descriptive Charts I — VI

As a way of complementing the statistics, this chapter uses case material, derived from a closer examination of 12 families. These families were randomly selected in terms of their level of functioning. Six were rated as functioning in the higher range and six as functioning in the lower range. Through this closer analysis something of the life style of these families was revealed. It must be recalled that since all of these families had been assessed by the agency and screened by agency procedures, they are a highly selected group. Nevertheless, a search for an understanding of the qualities that have enabled them to move ahead, to consolidate their gains and to prepare their children for a better life than they had is productive.

An examination of the 12 families, as described in Charts I through VI, showed them to have many characteristics in common. For example, despite an income range of $5500 to $19,000, with a median income of $7800, all were buying homes in the city of Philadelphia, seven of which were in racially mixed neighborhoods and five in a segregated ghetto. The homes were described by the research interviewers as in "fair" to "good" repair; "moderately clean" to "spotless," and "adequately furnished" to "well-furnished." No home reflected disorganization or poor housekeeping capacity. Although it is not uncommon for black wives to work, it attests to the stable, home-centered quality of these 12 families that eight of the wives are full-time housewives. Two wives have part-time work. Two wives could be described as career women, one of whom, a teacher, earned more than her husband. It could be speculated that whereas many middle-class wives feel "liberated" by holding a job outside the home, the wives in this group might enjoy freedom from the necessity of such employment.

Of the husbands in the group, five had 12 or more years of schooling, six had reached tenth grade or less, one had too little formal schooling to specify in terms of grade level. Although a recent government report stated that blacks are "more likely to be . . . finishing high school and college than they were a decade ago,"[1] the husbands in this group were not of an age to have profited by the educational opportunities of the last decade. Only two men were under 40, the median age being 46. Despite limited educations most had achieved a certain economic security, chiefly in semiskilled blue-collar jobs or white-collar clerical work. Their occupations included those of barber, truck driver, rubber worker, security guard, steel mill worker, clerk, gas works operator, laborer in a city department, welder, and assistant school principal. Five of the husbands had been reared in urban areas. Seven had emigrated from the south, with the attendant readjustments from rural to urban living.

From the point of view of housing and income, however, these families were well described by the government report quoted earlier, which continued: ". . . important gains by Negroes in earlier years in their level of living have been retained and in most instances have been increased. They are more likely to be receiving higher incomes, holding better jobs, living in better housing. . . . About one out of every three families of Negro and other races had an income of $8000 or more in 1968."[2]

These are the characteristics which the 12 families, regardless of placement method, shared. One difference between the six traditional and six quasi-adoption families was the tendency for the latter to be older (see Tables 11 and 12). A still more interesting fact was that of those families rated in the lower range of functioning, all were in the older age groups. Eight of these were quasi- and one a traditional adoption family. It follows that those rated in the higher range of functioning were somewhat younger. Another difference might be noted on "Perception of Marital Functioning." Five families, four quasi and one traditional, in the lower range of functioning felt that their marriages were less than satisfactory. Although these differences are of interest from the point of view of case material, they were not statistically significant.

In all the families, with the exception of the K.s, the parents projected a high degree of parental satisfaction, warmth and affection for the child. It may be that this capacity to project warmth and acceptance accounted in large part for the fact that only 10 families in the total study were rated as functioning in the lower range. Other factors, such as the success these families were achieving in their upward mobility, their concern for the child, and the aura of home-centeredness, all highly acceptable to a team of interviewers made up of social workers, psychologists and educators, may account for the preponderance of families rated as functioning in the higher range. Because of the overall similarities between the quasi- and the traditional adoption families and the lack of clear-cut difference between those rated in the higher and lower ranges of functioning, the case illustrations will be given without reference to method of adoption or rating category.

Early Life Experiences

Since only two husbands in the 12 families accompanied wife and child for the office interview, the responses are chiefly descriptive of the experiences of the wives. Of the 14 parents who were interviewed, 12 mothers and two fathers, only five grew up in intact homes. Of the other nine, four were reared by the mother, the father having died or deserted, and five by father and stepmother, or grandparents, or family friend. Yet with one exception all of them remembered their childhood as having been either "moderately happy" or "very happy." The exception had lost both parents by the time he was 6, then lived with his grandparents, both of whom were dead by the time he was 12, from which age he managed pretty much on his own. He recalled his childhood as "moderately unhappy."

Despite the fact that these 14 parents grew up during depression years, when economic conditions for blacks were much less opportune than in the last decade, all but one stated that they had had "adequate" to "plenty" of food and clothing and "adequate" housing. When given a choice between "I always had enough" or "I never had much," ten chose the first statement, only four the second. The majority said they loved their parents or surrogate parents and felt loved by them. To do as well for their children as their parents did "and something better" is a theme that stands out in the tapes and ratings.

In view of the circumstances, the absence of ambivalent or critical comments and the flat denial of deprivation or rejection are difficult to understand. Various explanations, however, are worth mentioning. The measurement scale (Schedule V) may have been constructed in a simplistic "either — or" fashion, which provided too little choice of response. Again, the respondents may have answered out of an idealization of their parents or, perhaps, denied or repressed experiences that were painful. On the other hand, these families may have felt that their parents did the best they could under the circumstances, so that what they received of the basic necessities was truly valued, perhaps because of the warmth with which it was given.

From the taped interviews, it was clear that the parents responded to questions in regard to "early life experiences" with brief answers and little spontaneity.

1. Mrs. L.'s father died when she was 4. She lived with her mother, who remarried when Mrs. L. was 14. Her stepfather died a year later. Mrs. L. had no memory of her father and little feeling about or relationship with her stepfather. When Mrs. L. was 16 her mother died, following which time she lived with a sister until her own marriage at 21. She has no memories before the age of 12.

In describing her childhood, Mrs. L. said, "I wasn't really happy, and I wasn't really unhappy. I guess I was moderately happy." She was lonely and missed her father. She felt that she had sufficient "food, clothing and housing" and that her mother had "genuinely loved" her. When given a choice of "I always had enough" or "I never had much," she chose the latter. She would not want her child to "go through" what she did.

2. Mrs. G., who, at the age of 5 lost her mother, had a still more distressing and unhappy childhood. By the time she was 18 she had changed homes at least eight times. Her father, after the death of her mother, married three times. Each time he had a home, he took Mrs. G. to live with him, where she felt tolerated by the stepmothers. Twice the home was broken up by the death of the stepmother and in the interim periods Mrs. G. lived with Miss Mabel, a family friend, with an uncle, and with a sister. Although there was a successive loss of mother figures, Mrs. G.'s father remained a constant figure in her life. She spoke of him with affection.

Mrs. G. had no memory of her mother and in recalling her childhood stated that she had blocked out a great deal. She thought she had been "moderately happy," had had plenty of "food, clothing and housing" and that in general she had "always had enough." She expressed confidence that she could "manage" and felt that "people liked her" because she liked them. She would be "satisfied to do as well" for her children as her father did for her.

As has been mentioned, most of the 14 parents who answered Schedule V expressed a love of their parents. Appreciation of how the parents had to struggle to maintain the family is vividly revealed by two of the mothers:

3. Mrs. F. remembered back to the age of 4 or 5 and despite being reared in a poverty area during a depression, recalled the family's celebrating birthdays and holidays with "big dinners" and "the family around." From the age of 5 or 6, Mrs. F. lived with her mother and three siblings because for economic reasons her father had to leave the family. "My father was there for a while. . . . He couldn't get a job. My mother had to go on relief. . . . A man wasn't allowed in the house. . . . He told us he was going away to get work . . . they were separated for years. The long separation really broke them up."

Mrs. F. thought she was "moderately happy" as a child, but "my mother always had to work (after a period on relief) . . . couldn't be with us as much as we would have liked. . . . It was sad." Mrs. F. felt she had "adequate food and clothing" and stressed that they had never lived in an apartment, but had always had a house. She felt her parents loved her. "I think my mother loved us very dearly . . . She worked hard for us . . . I couldn't see her as much as I would have liked." Mrs. F. thought her father showed his love for his family by leaving them to enable her mother to obtain relief funds. Despite very few material things there was warmth. "One of the things my mother stressed in our house was that we love one another. We were close." Mrs. F. felt she had "enough" according to what could be expected, but she hopes her children will not have to experience a depression. "I was raised in poverty."

4. Mrs. C. grew up in a family of eight children; her family was "extremely poor." . . . She did not have the material things her son has. But she did have love. . . "There was closeness" . . . but she always thought "it must be wonderful to be an only child and get anything you want." When a child she did not realize "how happy we were" compared with other families.

Later Experiences

Schedule VI asked for examples of positive, neutral or restricting later experiences and examples of people who were a positive, neutral or negative influence in modifying their early childhood backgrounds. The most frequent positive experience was the church, named by 13. Twelve parents named their marriage as a positive influence. Next in order were work, nine, and education, eight. However, clubs and organizations were mentioned by five parents. These covered working for civil rights groups, belonging to the Masons, enjoying sports, sewing, and being president of a choral group. Negative and restrictive experiences included being downgraded by a teacher for being black; having a chronic health problem; derogatory comments about an adopted daughter's "not being pretty"; the many years spent in caring for a mother-in-law; not having had more schooling.

People who represented a positive influence were listed in this order: spouse, 12; minister, 11; employer, nine; relative, nine; close friend, eight. Two parents, Mrs. G. and Mrs. L., did not consider their spouses positive people in their lives. Mr. D., who had grown up "pretty much as an orphan," felt his in-laws were a positive influence. Mrs. B. was grateful to a godmother for enabling her to take piano lessons. Two parents said their adoption worker had been a positive influence. Only four parents viewed neighbors as important to them.

It is of interest that the parents listed many positive experiences and helpful people, but only five that were negative and restrictive, two of these experiences being racially related.

Parental Description of the Child (Schedule III)

Of the 24 parents in this subsample, including both fathers and mothers, as described in Charts I — VI, only one mother (Mrs. K.) expressed serious dissatisfaction with her child. A number of parents were concerned that their child was too passive and compliant; two mothers thought the child was too destructive. In general, these parents described their children as normal and healthy, with a few mild problems with which they felt able to cope. The family in which the mother complained of the daughter's defiance subsequently applied to the agency for postadoption counseling.

A positive, giving quality in these families is evidenced clearly in their own comments about their children.

5. The T.s' satisfaction in their 4-year-old son, their acceptance and love of him comes across emphatically and without ambivalence. Mrs. T. described "more happiness" since adopting; she is "satisfied" with everything about him; there is "nothing disappointing" about him; could "not feel different about him if own child"; "in all ways is like my own child"; "between Michael and me there is a close relationship". Mr. T. sums up his son as follows: "He's a pretty normal child, you know. He's more a normal child than the average child. He sleeps all night. When he gets up he always speaks. He eats well; when he comes to the table he says a little blessing. He says his prayers before he goes to bed." Mr. T. enjoys everything about rearing his son, ". . . taking him to ballgames and different places. In other words, he's just a light in the home, that's all."

Both parents describe Michael as a loving, friendly child and if they would admit to any slight criticism, it would be that he is inclined to be "a follower" and "too friendly" outside the home. Mrs. T. thinks he picked up being friendly from her. Mr. T. described the way Michael likes to cross his legs as his father does. He stated that sometimes Michael gets on his nerves: "He likes to climb all over me . . . or get up on my leg and play rodeo like on television. Sometimes after a hard day's work it gets on my nerves." Both parents describe Michael as "all boy."

6. Mrs. F. described great satisfaction with her 4-year-old daughter, a child placed at 18 months of age who measured "bright normal." "From the very beginning she was our child. . . . She looked like me. I came from a large family, always had children

around me. I've had five boys. . . . I love my daughter very much." An additional source of satisfaction is that Vera "is intelligent; she comprehends quickly. I like this. I've never had a difficult time with Vera. She respects my authority as a mother."

Mr. F. projected an equally keen sense of satisfaction as a parent. "She's only a 4-year-old girl. I don't think she should be any problem to us . . . she's a happy child. She wants a lot of attention; sometimes she asks for help with something she can do in order to get attention. I give her attention but I make her do it. I don't stand around to spoil the child. Sometimes I have to crack down on her."

"She's a real friendly child; in fact, I think things will come easy to her in life; she's powerful friendly. I took her to the zoo Sunday. She was going out of her way to be friendly . . . she's just that way."

Mr. F. described the way some of the children in the neighborhood "mistreat" her by taking her toys and candy. "We try to explain to her that not all people will speak to her or be nice to her or like her."

Caseworker's Evaluation of the Attitudes of Adoptive Parents Toward Adoption, Their Child (Schedule IV)

With the exception of one mother, Mrs. K., all of the 24 parents are rated high on this scale. The ratings of 3-4-5 represent the impressions of the research interviewers on the following items: Satisfaction in Parental Role; Acceptance of Adoptive Role; Ease of Parental Communication With Child About Adoption; Parental Warmth and Affection Toward Child; Child Rearing. There was less consistency of rating on the third and last items.

Again, letting the parents speak for themselves provides the best way of illustrating these ratings:

7. Mr. and Mrs. G. were rated high (4 and 5) in Satisfaction in Parental Role. Mr. G. liked having "somebody around the house." He quoted his wife as saying "Kevin talks like me and walks like me." Mrs. G. feels they have most fun as a family when they go together on vacations. Her husband "works hard"; when "he's home he's tired." Mrs. G. also stated she still "can't realize (she) is a mother."

Mr. and Mrs. G. were rated high-average (4) in Acceptance of Adoptive Role. They were not concerned about background or heredity. In Communication about Adoption, the G.s were average (3), for they were apprehensive about using the word "adopted" and discussing his adoptive status. Mrs. G. stated she would tell the child if he asked. They were rated average (3) (Mr. G.) to high-average (4) (Mrs. G.) in Warmth and Affection. Mr. G. might overdo buying things for Kevin to show his affection and Mrs. G. can, at times, be quite harsh. In Child Rearing they were rated high-average (4), for they agreed on most things and tended to back up each other. When they disagreed, Mr. G. tended to give in. "Let's face it, with a woman and a kid, you have to go along with the program" (laughter). But Mrs. G. wished her husband would not leave most of the disciplining to her.

8. Mr. and Mrs. C. were rated high (5) in Satisfaction in Parental Role. Mr. C. confirmed his wife's statement that they enjoy being together as a family. "My wife and I were married quite a while before deciding to adopt. My wife was getting pretty bored.

After we got A. it helped a lot. . . . For fun, we like to go to the shore, go visiting, ride in the park together."

Both parents were rated high (4 and 5) in Acceptance of Adoptive Role. A. is living up to their expectations. Each expressed a wish that he would grow up to be a leader. They felt that at age 5, he tends to be a follower. Since adopting A. they have learned that two neighbors have adopted. "They came to us, wished us the best of luck." The C.s feel "real bad" if A. is criticized by anyone. "I guess any parent would. We feel more tender about him, I guess, than if he was born to us." Both parents feel he resembles them in appearance and personality.

Both parents are rated high (4 and 5) in Communication About Adoption. Mrs. C. had "told A. many times about his adoption. When he's older, if he asks about his other mother, I'll have to answer him. . . . I will say he has just one mother . . . that other lady. That doesn't sound right either. So I have a problem how to answer."

As to Parental Warmth and Affection, Mr. and Mrs. C. again are rated high (4 and 5). Mrs. C. asked, "How could you not show affection to a child you love?" She vividly described physical affection. Mr. C. said A. likes to sit close to him. "He puts his arms around me. I hug him, too. He's a very affectionate boy. He kisses his mother, but we shake hands. I tell him he's a big boy now."

In Child Rearing, both Mr. and Mrs. C. were rated high (5) in compatibility in decision making. Both feel that they share in discipline and decisions by "talking things out." As to who does the disciplining, Mr. C. stated, "It all depends on when he does something wrong. We usually agree. We may send him to his room or spank his hands. It makes a child mean to beat him. If we disagree, we don't want A. to hear."

Perception of Marital Functioning

9. Mrs. G. believed they are "too old" for open displays of affection. She neither expected nor wanted much, but she also felt they have companionship and understanding. She was very dissatisfied with their sex relations, feeling they have never been compatible. He was demanding and "too rough"; she usually "doesn't feel like being bothered." Mrs. G. believed this is the state of affairs with most couples, so "it's what (she) expects." In discussing both the affectional and sexual aspects of their marriage, Mr. G. was taciturn. He was "satisfied"; their relationship was "OK."

10. Mrs. K., in the office interview, described with sadness the sense of isolation she felt in her marriage. The interviewer noted these statements: "They care about each other, but neither is demonstrative. They don't have much time together; both are busy and frequently tired. They work out compromises with little friction. There is little time for fun together as a family, but they talk over most everything and share feelings and ideas easily."

11. By contrast with the K.s, Mr. and Mrs. D. perceived their marriage as important and helpful to them both. Each experienced a very disrupted early life. Mr. D. never knew his father and his mother died when he was 6. Subsequently he lived with grandparents for 2 or 3 years and godparents for a few years. As he stated, he had a "rough life" in which he "managed to eke out an existence." He described his wife as not just a wife, but father and mother as well.

Mrs. D.'s father died when she was 2 years old and from the age of 10 she had numerous "live-in" jobs. She returned to her mother's home on weekends.

In describing their marriage, Mrs. D. said they made a real effort to please each other; they managed their money together, did almost everything together and worked out compromises if differences arose. She felt they had a strong sense of sharing and understanding.

Mr. D.'s responses were brief and constricted and his attitude one of sadness. The interviewer felt he was trying in his marriage to compensate for the early deprivation and succeeding to a limited extent.

Comments Regarding Family Functioning

All but one parent in this group of 24 projected a high degree of warmth and acceptance of their children. However, in some of these families there are factors that may not bode well for the future adjustment of parents and child. Mr. and Mrs. K. give little emotional support to each other, are divided in their marriage and disagree about child rearing. This state of affairs encourages their daughter to divide the parents further through manipulative behavior. Whereas Mrs. K. criticized their daughter, Mr. K. defended her. Fortunately, both parents have asked for counseling for their many relationship problems.

Mr. and Mrs. D. are a family who, despite serious early deprivation, limited education and a marginal income of $5900, are struggling to achieve and maintain security and family unity. They migrated to Philadelphia from a Southern state 7 years before their application to adopt in 1964. At that time, Mr. D. earned $60 a week as a janitor and Mrs. D. earned $10 a day as a domestic. Despite a marginal income, they chose the traditional rather than quasi-adoption plan. Over a 5-year period, Mr. D. has found a better paying job, supports his family and is buying a home.

Mr. D., preferring to forget his "orphan-like" early life, listed military service, church, the Masons and his marriage as positive influences. When talking about himself, Mr. D.'s comments were sad, constricted and brief. In talking about his marriage and child, he spoke of how much he enjoys being with his wife and child. He was open-minded about adoption education, reflective about his role as a father and aware of the importance of the parents giving support to each other in child rearing.

These parents derive a great deal of satisfaction from their son, but there are indications that they may be infantilizing and overindulging him. Both parents find it difficult to limit him. At 5 he has severe enuresis. Mrs. D. has a great need to "mother," and "mothers" both son and husband. Her emphasis is upon giving and "feeding" rather than encouraging independence and emotional growth. Both parents tend to use the child to help overcome their feelings of deprivation.

Mr. and Mrs. L. are another family who experienced forms of deprivation. In Mrs. L.'s instance, there was emotional deprivation due to the loss of her father when she was 4. Her response indicated a sense of loneliness. She had a mother who provided a home. . . . "I loved my mother because she loved me." She described her mother as old-fashioned, perhaps implying strict and repressive. Mr. L. stated that his parents were in "some ways strict," keeping their children "under control."

Mr. and Mrs. L. are loyal to their parents, displaying a realistic appreciation of the social and economic conditions with which their parents struggled. They may regard strict parents as caring parents, but there are indications of ways in which earlier deprivation may impair their overall functioning: Mrs. L. is needy for love and attention, is overly possessive and controlling of her son and too passive in her relationship with her husband. Mrs. L. summed up her thoughts about her marriage in this way: "We have our ups and downs, but no separations. We work it out. I don't think I could ask for much more than that. I couldn't and I wouldn't." As their son grows older and separating experiences such as school occur, Mrs. L. may again feel lonely. She could become more competitive with her husband for the boy's affections and attention. If so, there is a possibility the marriage will suffer; Mr. L. expressed some dissatisfaction with it.

Mr. and Mrs. G., like the L.s, are older parents, fairly routinized in their marital organization and communication, who project themselves on tape and in the research material more as grandparents or older foster parents than parents. There is a high degree of warmth and affection and acceptance of the child. The child is much valued both for himself and for what he does to enliven an otherwise fairly dull home life. Both the G.s and L.s will provide stability, security and consistent care to their children.

However, both families tend to be overly indulgent, the L.s more than the G.s. Mrs. G. undoubtedly needs Kevin's companionship to fill a void in her marriage. With resignation, she described how little they do together except for traveling together on vacations. Her husband "is always at the club." They talk about "practically everything," but Mrs. L. stated this with boredom and dissatisfaction. "He doesn't say anything. Whatever I say is all right with him." Mr. G.'s attitude was that this state of affairs was satisfactory to him. Mrs. G. complained of Kevin's constant demands for her attention. Yet she also welcomed it. He helped her to feel alive. In the taped home interview, Mrs. G. described how Kevin "likes to have his own way" and of how he prodded her, "Mommy, get mad. When you going to get mad?" She suspected he often did things to "get (her) mad." She would express irritation with Kevin's demands for attention, but in the next sentence say, "I sure do love him."

Except for Kevin, Mrs. G. is a lonely woman, resigned and somewhat depressed. She feels toward her husband much as she felt toward her father and a succession of mother people. There is denial of the pain of loss and separation, and gratitude for any semblance of caring and attention. As with Mrs. L., this is about all she expects.

Mr. G. may be representative of the blue-collar pattern. A man works to provide financially for his family, but his social life is lived outside the home in pubs and taverns with male cronies. Except for his role as breadwinner, he takes a fairly passive role in family decisions and discipline of the child. He neither asks much nor gives much of himself in a relationship with his wife and child. He has found a way of life that is satisfying to him and his denial defenses protect him from the impact of his wife's dissatisfactions.

It can be speculated that as the boys in these two families grow older and undertake separating experiences through school and friends, both Mrs. G. and Mrs. L. will become more depressed and dissatisfied. This kind of behavior may drive the husbands farther away, resulting in a divisiveness in the family that will force the growing youngsters to choose between their parents or to choose neither in favor of friends.

By contrast, two other families described in considerable detail present a different picture of their marriage and themselves. Mrs. C. feels her marriage has helped her broaden and expand. She and her husband have many friends in common, help each other in daily activities, "talk everything over." Mrs. C. is a professional career woman, earning more than her husband. On tape, she speaks of her husband with respect; both convey a feeling of enjoyment of each other and satisfaction in their shared responsibilities. They are open-minded in questioning how they will help their son understand his adoption status.

Mr. and Mrs. F. convey an even stronger sense of a satisfying give and take in their marriage. Mrs. F. states on tape: "He's a very important part of my life. When I make boo-boos, he can relate to me in a very positive way. . . . We both enjoy sex."

She expressed respect for her husband in this fashion: "When there is disagreement about money (or what she has spent), he takes away my charge accounts until the budget is balanced."

The F.s project themselves as a lively, verbal couple who have achieved a satisfying give and take in their marriage. In listening to their taped interviews, a joie de vivre quality comes across. In the previous study of adoption family functioning, superior family functioning was described in this way: " . . . the outstanding (quality) being joie de vivre. The parents appeared highly compatible and cooperated in providing the children with warm educative care."[3]

Mrs. C. was working as a homemaker for a social agency at the time of their initial application for a child in 1965. As her husband's income increased from $5600 to $9000 in a 4-year period, she no longer chose to work and expressed enjoyment in being a full-time housewife. She also engaged in community activities. Mr. and Mrs. C. conveyed a sense of a warm, casual, intimate life style for their children and a satisfying libidinal relationship for themselves.

Their adequate self-esteem and more open personalities also are related to their attitudes about their child and about her adoption. Mrs. C. explained how each night she would say, "I am very glad I adopted you," until Vera said, "Why do you always use that word, Mommy?" "So I stopped." Mrs. C. described how their local bank presented her with roses when she told the staff of Vera's placement. Neither she nor Mr. C. are secretive about adoption, either in the home or in their community. They have confidence that they can help Vera understand her special place in their home.

B. CHILD FACTORS

General Characteristics and Descriptive Charts VII and VIII

This subsample consists of eight boys and four girls who at the time of their adoption placement ranged in age from 5 to 28 months, with a median age of 17 months. At the time of the research examination they ranged in age from 4 years, 4 months to 6 years, 9 months, with a median age of 5 years, 11 months. Only one child, a 6½-year-old boy, placed in the H. home when 28 months old, was considered to be maximally deprived. Six children were moderately deprived; five were minimally deprived. It was known that six biological mothers had had prenatal care. In six instances there was either no prenatal care or no information.

Nine children had had one placement, i.e., were in one foster home from early infancy to the time of the adoption placement. Three children had had two placements. Of the total group, only one child was with his natural mother during the first few months of his life.

60

Psychological Ratings and Evaluating Comments

At the time of the research examination, nine children tested average to above average and bright-normal. Three children tested below average. In comparing the research test scores with the earlier appraisal of the child's development, there is remarkable consistency. In only two cases was there a marked change. The maximally deprived boy placed with the H. family tested low-average when 2 years of age. Despite a history of meningitis and a number of behavior problems in his adoption home, this boy at 6½ years tested average, with a range between 4½- and 8-year items.

The other child, a 4-year 8-month-old boy, placed with the J. family when 7 months old, was then considered to be high-average in development. He was rated borderline to low-average by the research psychologist (see Chart VIII). The only significant clues are in the child's early history, in that he had an Apgar rating of 1 at birth and needed aspiration. He was described as a hyperactive, restless, tense baby with some distractability and disinterest and a moderate attention span prior to his adoption placement. As indicated on Chart IV, the J. parents were rated as average to high on items 1, 2 and 4 of Scale IV with respect to Satisfaction in Parental Role, Acceptance of Adoptive Role and Parental Warmth and Affection.

It is in reviewing the psychologist's *Evaluative Comments* that the indications of difficulties in parental functioning and child adjustment receive considerable substantiation. Six families were described as too indulgent, overprotective and inconsistent in child rearing, with consequent immaturities in the child. Two of these families, the B.s and the F.s, were providing stimulation toward learning to the child but, at the same time, were aware that they were fostering immature behavior through overindulgence. One family, the A.s, in combination with the school, had too high expectations and were exerting overly strict controls. The child, a boy of 6 years, 8 months, was an anxious child, preoccupied with fire. This family and three others were advised to obtain special help from the agency or another source. Two of the three families have been described in case illustrations of Mr. and Mrs. G. and Mr. and Mrs. K., who are receiving post-adoption counseling. Mr. and Mrs. H., who are rearing the maximally deprived boy who had meningitis, have been working with the agency in a close, continuous way since the time of placement. This is a family who continue to receive a large number of services from the agency in order to bolster their care of a traumatized and very needy child.

The research psychologist confirmed impressions of the social work interviewers that Mr. and Mrs. D. are very indulgent of their son, tending to infantilize him. Mrs. D. calls him her "baby." But the child himself, described as nervous and tense, may have been revealing a source of trouble in his Doll Play when he acted out a father beating his child. It may be possible that Mr. D., who suffered severe deprivation and prefers to forget about it, who needs his wife to mother him, may not handle his frustrations and tensions in an adult way. This is the kind of interaction that could be expected, but that was not revealed in the home or office interviews.

CHART I

FAMILY FACTORS

HIGHER RANGE OF FUNCTIONING

FAMILY	SERVICE	AGES AT TIME OF RESEARCH		EDUCATION IN GRADES		INCOME		OCCUPATION		BUYING HOME	RENTING	CONDITION OF HOME
		H	W	H	W	H	W	H	W			
A. Family	QA	39	43	12	12	13,000	occas. works at $65 a week	Skilled blue collar	Semi-skilled	8 rooms in middle-class racially mixed neighborhood	No	Good repair; moderately clean; well-furnished
B. Family	Trad.	43	39	10	12	10,000	10,000	Skilled blue collar	Supervisory	6 rooms in middle-class racially mixed neighborhood	No	Good repair; moderately clean; adequate furnishings
C. Family	Trad.	41	41	12	18	5,500	10,000	Skilled blue collar	Prof.	6 rooms in racially mixed, middle-class neighborhood	No	Good repair; spotless; well-furnished
D. Family	Trad.	44	42	Little formal schooling	Little formal schooling	5,900	0	Semi-skilled laborer	HW	6 rooms in lower-class ghetto	No	Good repair; moderately clean; well-furnished
E. Family	QA	36	36	18	12	19,000 (8,000 when app.)	0	Prof.	HW	6 rooms in segregated upper middle-class neighborhood	No	Good repair; spotless; well-furnished
F. Family	QA	45	44	12	12	9,000	0	Skilled blue collar	HW	8 rooms in segregated, middle-class neighborhood	No	Fair repair; moderately clean; well-furnished

CHART II

FAMILY FACTORS

HIGHER RANGE OF FUNCTIONING

FAMILY	EARLY CHILDHOOD EXPERIENCE		ATTITUDES TOWARD CHILDHOOD EXPERIENCE		ATTITUDES TOWARD PARENTS	
	H	W	H	W	H	W
A. Family		Lived with both parents until 20. One sibling.		Very happy; plenty of food, clothing, housing. Parents loved her. Always had enough.		Loved both parents. Doesn't want her children to go through what she did with parents.
B. Family		Reared by mother; parents separated when 3. One sib.		Mod. happy; adequate food, clothing, housing. Mother was overprotective; always had enough.		Loved her mother; will be satisfied if she can do as well for her child.
C. Family		Lived with both parents until 18. Had 7 siblings.		Mod. happy; plenty to adequate food, clothing, housing. Always had enough.		Loved her parents; will be satisfied if can do as well for children.
D. Family	Mother died when 6. Never knew father. Lived with grandpar. 3 yrs. and godparents "few" yrs. Felt like an orphan.	Lived with mother. Father died when 2. Had numerous live-in jobs from age of 10 but saw mother frequently.	Mod. unhappy. Managed to eke out an existence. Rough life; prefers to forget it. Never had much.	Very happy but regrets did not know father. Had plenty of food, clothing and housing. Always had enough.	Loved his godparents. Doesn't want his child to go through what he did.	Loved her mother. Tries to do as her mother did.
E. Family		Grew up in an intact family.		Very happy; adequate food and housing; plenty of clothes. Always had enough. Feels people like her.		Loved mother; disappointed in father; he gave little to children.
F. Family		Reared by mother. Father left home for economic reasons when she was 6.		Mod. happy; adequate food, clothing, housing. Always had enough. Feels people like her.		Loved her parents; felt they loved her.

FAMILY FACTORS

CHART III

HIGHER RANGE OF FUNCTIONING

FAMILY	RATING OF CHILD'S BEHAVIOR	CASEWORKER'S EVAL. OF ATTITUDES TOWARD ADOPTION AND CHILD	MARITAL FUNCTIONING	RESPONSE TO INTERVIEW
A. Family	Both parents described 6-year-old son as normal, healthy child with few mild problems.	Rated high (5) in items 1-4; about average (3) in child rearing. Wife feels husband is too lenient in child rearing. He does not support her method of discipline.	Wife feels has a satisfactory marriage.	Warm, responsive
B. Family	5-year-old boy described as normal, healthy child with few mild problems.	Parents rated high (4) to (5) on all items.	Wife feels they have a good marriage.	Warm, responsive
C. Family	Both parents gave positive rating; described a few mild problems in 5-year-old son.	Both parents rated average to high in all 5 items.	Wife is very satisfied in her marriage.	Warm, responsive
D. Family	Parents were in agreement in describing a passive, compliant child, inclined to be fearful. Few specific problems.	Parents rated average to high.	Average to high on all items for both. However, father appears lonely and unhappy.	Anxious, tense
E. Family	Parents rated child as normal, without problems except for greediness for food and lying to avoid punishment.	Parents rated high on all items.	Wife feels has very satisfactory marriage. Wishes husband could be home more.	Warm, responsive
F. Family	Parents rated child as normally assertive, independent, generally compliant, careful of toys, often not cautious enough in new situations. Jealous of younger children.	Parents rated high in all areas.	Wife feels they have a very satisfactory marriage.	Warm, responsive

CHART IV

FAMILY FACTORS

LOWER RANGE OF FUNCTIONING

FAMILY	SERVICE	AGES AT TIME OF RESEARCH		EDUCATION IN GRADES		INCOME		OCCUPATION		BUYING HOME	RENT-ING	CONDITION OF HOME
		H	W	H	W	H	W	H	W			
G. Family	QA	51	52	10	11	$7,800	0	Semi-skilled	HW	7 rooms; racially mixed, lower-class neighborhood	No	Good repair; spotless; adequate furnishings
H. Family	QA	46	46	10	10	7,800	0	Semi-skilled	HW	6 rooms; racially mixed, middle-class neighborhood	No	Fair repair; moderately clean; well-furnished
I. Family	QA	52	53	9	8	7,000	0	Skilled	HW	8 rooms; ghetto neighborhood	No	Fair repair; moderately clean; well-furnished
J. Family	QA	48	42	16 (did not receive college degree)	12	8,000	0	White collar	HW	6 rooms; in ghetto; middle-class	No	Good repair; moderately clean; adequate furnishings
K. Family	QA	56	43	8	HS (1 yr. coll.)	5,500	0	Skilled	HW	6 rooms; racially mixed, lower-class neighborhood	No	Good repair; moderately clean; adequate furnishings
L. Family	Trad.	51	44	7	10	7,000	$18 for 2 days	Semi-skilled	Part-time domestic	8 rooms; racially mixed, middle-class neighborhood	No	Good repair; spotless; well-furnished

CHART V

FAMILY FACTORS

LOWER RANGE OF FUNCTIONING

FAMILY	EARLY CHILDHOOD EXPERIENCE		ATTITUDES TOWARD CHILDHOOD EXPERIENCE		ATTITUDES TOWARD PARENTS	
	H	W	H	W	H	W
G. Family	Lived with both parents until adult. Had 1 brother died in infancy.	Mother died when 5. Reared by 3 step-mothers and family friend.	Very happy; plenty of food, clothing. Always had enough.	Mod. happy; plenty of food, clothing, housing. Always had enough.	Parents loved him and he them. Will be satisfied if can do as well for child.	Felt family friend loved her. Neutral toward stepmothers.
H. Family		Mother died when 8. Father remarried. Grew up with father and stepmother.		Mod. happy; plenty of food, clothing, housing. Always had enough.		Closer to her step-mother. Felt both parents loved her.
I. Family		Father died when an infant. Reared by aunt until 14, then lived with mother – 4 sibs.		Mod. happy; plenty to adequate food, clothing, housing. Never had much.		Loved her aunt and uncle.
J. Family		Mother died when 5. Father reared her. 5 siblings.		Mod. happy; plenty of food, clothing, housing. Always had enough.		Did not feel loved by father but loved him.
K. Family		Reared in intact family. 9 sibs.		Moderately happy; plenty of food, clothing. Insufficient housing. Always had enough. People like her. (Worker felt denying.)		Loved both parents. They loved her.
L. Family		Father died when 4; mother when 16. Had stepfather for 1 yr. at age 14. (No memories before 12.)		Mod. happy (lonely); plenty of food, clothing, housing. Never had much.		Loved mother; no memory of father. Neutral toward stepfather.

CHART VI

FAMILY FACTORS

LOWER RANGE OF FUNCTIONING

FAMILY	RATING OF CHILD'S BEHAVIOR	CASEWORKER'S EVAL. OF ATTITUDES TOWARD ADOPTION AND CHILD	MARITAL FUNCTIONING	RESPONSE TO INTERVIEW
G. Family	Parents described child as normal, but too compliant by father and destructive by mother. Mother had more complaints than father.	Parents rated average to high.	Wife neither expects nor wants much from husband. Is resigned to lack of affection. Both feel they have companionship and understanding. Few disagreements.	Anxious, tense during part of interview with both parents
H. Family	Parents described child as having moderately severe problems due to serious illness in infancy. Also described improvement in child.	Parents rated average to high.	Wife states she has nobody else. Sometimes satisfied in marriage, sometimes not. Husband often calls her "Mom." She manages money. He likes to be quiet.	Warm, responsive
I. Family	Parents rated 5-year-old child as normal except for extreme fussiness in eating; mentioned other problems such as fire setting, unusual sex interest, bedwetting and wanting her own way all the time.	Parents rated average to high in all items except child rearing (Item 5) (2). Father lets mother make all the decisions but feels she needs to be stricter.	Wife is rated low to average. Feels they have companionship rather than closeness and affection. Have separate bedrooms and separate interests.	Warm, responsive
J. Family	Parents described 4-year-old child as normal and without problems.	Parents rated average to high on all items. Father wishes he did not have to tell child he is adopted. Mother is in charge of children. Husband leaves decisions to her. He is too lenient.	Wife rates her marriage as very satisfactory in general. He is pillar of strength.	Hostile
K. Family	Mother complained of child's defiance. Father considered her usually compliant. Both parents felt she was indiscriminate in her interactions and too dominant. Very jealous child.	Mother has low degree of satisfaction as parent and reservations about adoption; father more middle of scale. Mother is average in warmth, father high. Father feels mother takes things too seriously.	Wife feels isolated from husband, neither demonstrative by nature. Don't do much together. Compromise on issues.	?
L. Family	Parents concerned about 4-year-old son's passivity and compliance. Mother felt he was destructive, whereas father considered him careful.	Parents rated high in satisfaction in parental role, acceptance of adoption and warmth and affection. Rated low in communication re adoption. Father rated low in child rearing; lets wife discipline.	Wife rated her marriage as high in satisfaction, father as average. He keeps some feelings to himself to avoid friction. Agree on finances.	Mother warm, responsive; father anxious, tense

Illustrations of Family Functioning   67

CHART VII

CHILD FACTORS
HIGHER RANGE OF FUNCTIONING

FAMILY	PARTICULARS ABOUT CHILD	DEGREE OF DEPRIVATION	COMMENTS ON SCHEDULE I RE CHILD'S EARLY EXPERIENCES	PSYCHOLOGIST'S RATINGS AND COMMENTS
A. Family QA	Male placed at 17 mos. Examined at 6 yrs., 8 mos.	Moderate	Incomplete data re birth and early development. With bio-mother until 8 mos. of age. Weighed 12 lbs., 8 oz. and could not sit up when admitted to care. Blossomed in foster home. Average in development.	Anxious boy, testing average, preoccupied with fire. Parents expect too much of boy. School very strict. Suggested postadoption counseling.
B. Family Trad.	Male placed at 24 mos. Examined at 6 yrs., 1 month.	Minimal	Child's development was normal and without problem; in one foster home from few days of age to adoption placement. Warm, accepting foster family. Considered high-average in development.	Child is bright; has vocabulary of 8-year-old. Emotionally more like a 5-year-old. However, mother felt child was easy to manage; home appears to provide stimulation.
C. Family Trad.	Male placed at 9 mos. Examined at 6 yrs., 9 mos.	Minimal	Child needed resuscitation at birth. Developed well. In one foster home from few days of age until adoption placement. Warm, accepting foster family. Considered average in development.	Child has vocabulary at 10-year level. More mature than many children his age. Testing bright-normal; receives much stimulation.
D. Family Trad.	Male placed at 11 mos. Examined at 5 yrs., 11 mos.	Moderate	Incomplete data re child's delivery. Bio-mother had no prenatal care. Child was in one foster home from early infancy, considered warm and accepting. Child developed slowly. Tested low-average.	Parents appear proud of son and unaware of his limitations. Testing low-average. Nervous, tense child. Has visual-motor problem. Mother "babies" child, calls him "my baby." Father denied physical punishment. In doll play, child acted out a father beating his child.
E. Family QA	Female placed at 20 mos. Examined at 6 yrs., 2 mos.	Moderate	Child had normal birth. Bio-mother had prenatal care. Child had early feeding problem and frequent URI infections. In one foster home from early infancy until adoption placement. Foster home was warm and accepting. Considered bright-normal.	Vocabulary above 8-year level; bright child who failed some tests because of inattention and not following directions. Mother confirmed child's willfulness and inattention at home and at school. Needs more peer relationships. Child has benefited from cultural stimulation. Suggested day camp.
F. Family QA	Female placed at 24 mos. Examined at 5 yrs., 1 month.	Moderate	Child had normal birth. Bio-mother had prenatal care. Was hospitalized for few days at 7 months for spitting and vomiting with one convulsion attack. In one foster home considered warm and accepting from early infancy until adoption placement, delayed for lack of a family. Considered to be bright-normal.	Child tested above average; has received abundant stimulation. Also somewhat indulged and overprotected. Mother urged to be more consistent in handling and expectations.

CHART VIII

CHILD FACTORS

LOWER RANGE OF FUNCTIONING

FAMILY	PARTICULARS ABOUT CHILD	DEGREE OF DEPRIVATION	COMMENTS ON SCHEDULE I RE CHILD'S EARLY EXPERIENCES	PSYCHOLOGIST'S RATINGS AND COMMENTS
G. Family QA	Male placed at 12 mos. Examined at 4 yrs., 5 mos.	Minimal	Child had normal birth. Bio-mother had prenatal care after 7th month. Child was in one foster home, a warm, accepting home, from birth. Agency considered child to be bright-normal	Child tested within average. May be brighter. Father had little interaction with child; mother complained of his demands for attention and his destructiveness. Suggested postadoption counseling.
H. Family QA	Male placed at 28 mos. Examined at 6 yrs., 6 mos.	Maximum	Child had normal birth; very little data re prenatal care. When 20 mos., child was hospitalized for 3 weeks with meningitis. Had two foster home placements; was a passive, floppy child who tested below average.	Child tested average with range of 4½ to 8 yr. items. Talkative and fairly cooperative. Mother reported marked lying, stealing, damaging toys and room, and defiance. Psychologist noted some immaturities but no pathology. Mother can feel overwhelmed, relies upon religion to alter misbehavior. Psychologist believes child can respond to reasonable limits and firm, gentle control. Advised parents to obtain special help.
I. Family QA	Female placed at 5 mos. Examined at 5 yrs., 6 mos.	Minimal	Child had normal birth; bio-mother had prenatal care. Was in one foster home; feeling tone in foster home neutral. Child vigorous, pleasant, considered average in development.	Child was responsive and likable; tested fully average with a range of 4.6 to 7. Punitive quality in her doll play. Mother did "practically all" of the talking. Father said little. Mother complained child dawdles over food, hates to go to bed, can be "willfully perverse." Mother did not appear to be warm and empathic with child.
J. Family QA	Male placed at 7 mos. Examined at 4 yrs., 8 mos.	Moderate	Child was full-term; normal delivery; respiration was induced; good recovery. No information re prenatal care. Child in one foster home, considered warm and accepting. He was thought to be high-average in development.	Child had bad cold, tested in borderline to low-average. Passed no items above 4 yr., 6 month level. Mother was aware of his slow capacity to learn, but not troubled or disappointed.
K. Family QA	Female placed at 12 mos. Examined at 4 yrs., 10 mos.	Minimal	Normal birth, no complications. No information re prenatal care. In one foster home (another agency). No information re kind of care. Was a healthy but overweight child. Average development.	Child tested above average, with a range 4.6 to 6 yr. level. Mother finds child hard to manage. Child is overactive, pushy and bossy. Post-adoption counseling suggested.
L. Family Trad.	Male placed at 20 mos. Examined at 4 yrs., 4 mos.	Moderate	Child had normal birth; bio-mother had prenatal care. Child had two foster home placements. Both considered warm and accepting. Child was a normally active, vigorous, contented child who appeared average in development.	Child tested within average with a range of 3 to 6 yr. level. Several indices of overindulgence. Parents well-meaning, but have some difficulty in understanding child behavior.

References

1. "The Social and Economic Status of Negroes in the United States," United States Department of Labor and Department of Commerce, 1969, vii.

2. *Ibid.,* vii.

3. Elizabeth A. Lawder *et al., A Followup Study of Adoptions: Post-Placement Functioning of Adoption Families, Vol. 1* (Child Welfare League of America, 1970), 123.

5

Implications for Practice

Theory

The literature contains important findings regarding the unloved and un-attached child. John Bowlby, Anna Freud, Renee Spitz, Jean Yarrow, Sally Provence, to name a few, have published their investigations of the effects of deprivation in early childhood. It is generally accepted that the earlier and more prolonged the absence of consistent, loving care for the infant and young child, the more serious the resulting emotional trauma. With long periods of deprivation, the child later has little or no capacity to love, to sense pain, joy or guilt, and may turn his aggression against himself as well as others.

Goals

The compelling goal of child placement is, therefore, the prevention, or failing that, the modification of the effects of trauma, both physical and psychological. It is to be noted in reference to this study that in comparison with children traditionally placed, the quasi children had more negative background factors. There were more foster home place-ments, longer stays in institutions and shelters during infancy, more abuse and neglect. In addition to a poorer start in life, there is indication of more negative constitutional factors. This group of children was, therefore, in danger unless something was done to counteract the effect of these circumstances.

With this in mind the quasi-adoption service was developed with a goal of providing a greater number of permanent homes for black infants and young children. Through the giving of a subsidy the number of placements was doubled during the 4 years covered by this study.

Service

It is difficult to determine whether the increase in adoption applications was due more to the innovative subsidy feature of the quasi-adoption program or to the publicity campaign, or to a combination of both. Because the agency had for many years publicized the plight of waiting children, it can be hypothesized that the feature of financial assistance was the more important factor, especially since the quasi-adoption families tended to be older, to have less income, and more natural children at home than was true of the traditional families. The fact that an administration of a practical service, the financial subsidy, was the only significant difference between the two groups in terms of services does not, however, negate the fact of service as an important aspect of the agency's work.

A variety of services was offered to both groups of parents, as is traditionally true of postplacement supervision of adoption families. Discussions covered aspects of child rearing, child health, development and stimulation, the adoption parents' feeling about the child and his background, the ascertaining of areas of anxiety or tension with respect to the child, plans for the child's schooling, and a philosophy about adoption education. Additionally, in terms of creating a favorable emotional climate for the child, casework service was available, when necessary, to the parents to help them recognize and resolve such friction and tension as might exist between them. Referral service, either to resources within the agency or the community, was available to any family member in connection with economic, educational or social problems. The fact that assistance in the areas of budget making and money management, of job training, of finding a better job, of obtaining better housing, and medical and dental care, was little sought may suggest, particularly in regard to money matters, the feeling of the parents that these were their own concern. Since a majority of the families listed the church and the minister as a major influence in their lives, they may traditionally turn to that resource in times of economic stress. However that may be, by means of ego-supportive measures, the staff did convey to the adopting families that, in addition to carrying out placement responsibilities for the child, the agency seeks a partnership with the family and stands ready to help when needed.

Placement Outcome

As has been previously pointed out, there were no statistically significant differences between the two groups of families. Children in both groups have a minimum of problems and are developing well. Their families are functioning with a good degree of warmth, affection, acceptance and satisfaction. Regardless of differences in education, employment and material goods, all have demonstrated the ability to cope relatively well with their respective realities. However, as might be expected, the outcome of placements with quasi-adoption families reflects the greater initial risk as well as less readiness on the part of families to complete adoption through court action. As of March 1, 1971, 70% of the quasi-adoption families had completed adoption, as compared with 97% completed adoptions by traditional adoption families. It should be noted, however, that the flexibility of the quasi-adoption program has allowed 90% of the children to remain with the original placement family.

72

Continuing Evaluation

Any innovative program must be carefully evaluated not only in terms of the initial assessment of families and children involved, but in foreseeing, given the circumstances, what problems may develop. As has been pointed out, both parents and children in the quasi-adoption group had more negative factors than was true of the traditional adoption families. In the cases where problems developed and the children were removed, it was felt that two qualities had not been properly assessed — the degree of depression in the woman and the degree of dependence in the man. As concerns the first point, it is not uncommon for a woman, if she is dissatisfied, lonely and depressed, to feel that a child will not only enliven the home but give meaning to her life. If, however, the depression has not resulted simply from changes in her situation (e.g., her children are now grown and require little of her), but is a reactivation of an earlier depression, the additional work and responsibility of a child may serve to deepen her depression. This, therefore, becomes an important diagnostic point.

The degree of dependence of the man is equally important. If he feels his relationship to his wife is threatened by the demands on her of a necessarily dependent child, the balance of the marriage is upset and the resulting unhappy atmosphere is unhealthful for all.

In addition to these points, there are important areas of child development that should be watched, specifically, those involved in separation. If the child has supplied the love and happiness that the woman sought, she may discourage his efforts to establish his independence. Problems may arise when he enters school and still more importantly in adolescence, when the teenager not only may encounter psychological difficulties, but when his presence may reactivate difficulties of his parents. Because of the age gap, reality tensions may build up between these much older parents and their adolescent child.

For these reasons the adoption needs to be seen by agency and parents alike as a continuum, with the resources of the agency available to all adoption families as the child in growing passes through the so-called "crisis" stages of adjustment and sometimes turbulence for both himself and his parents. Postadoptive counseling, increasingly used by white families but by only a few black families, can be extended as the latter learn of the service. Just as families commit themselves to a child through adoption, an agency needs to express its commitment to the family it helped to create not only through direct services but through such indirect services as arranging meetings of adoption families where common problems can be discussed, keeping them abreast of agency activities by mailing them agency literature, and involving them in recruitment efforts.

Summary

This is a study of a small, selected group of black families, half of whom adopted through a method traditionally used by Children's Aid Society of Pennsylvania and half through an innovative and subsidized program, which doubled at a relatively small cost the number of homes available for the permanent placement of black children. The parents in the quasi-adoption program were older, were less secure economically, and had less education and fewer job skills. The children placed with them, as compared with those placed in traditional adoption homes, had had more foster home placements, longer stays in institutions and shelters during infancy, more abuse and more neglect. Nevertheless, there were no statistically significant differences in the functioning of the two groups of parents nor in that of the two groups of children.

It was pointed out that in the quasi-adoption program, in which both children and parents had been subject to more than usual problems and pressure, some future problems could be anticipated. These were related to the introduction of a child into a home where the marriage was not altogether secure, because of either the degree of depression in the woman or the degree of dependence in the man, and to the problems of separation for both parents and child as the child's maturation led him to seek greater independence. In addition, the fact that in general the children in this group tested lower than those in the traditional families could mean greater pressure from the school on both child and family.

In conclusion: Children are not expendable; they require nuture, protection and stability to grow. Perhaps these ingredients in family life are more important today than ever before because of social upheaval and change that have not yet found a new balance. In a symbolic sense, the contribution of these families to children represents survival. Whether or not the families with whom we have placed children think in philosophical terms, they have chosen values that throughout the years have been tested and found vital to the well-being of children.

BIBLIOGRAPHY

Abrams, Charles. "The Housing Problem and the Negro." *Daedalus* 95: 64-76.

Anderson, J. W. "A Special Hell for Children in Washington." *Harper's Magazine* 231: 51-56.

Andrews, Roberta G. "Quasi-Adoption: A New Approach to the Permanent Placement of Negro Children." *Child Welfare* 47: 583-586.

_____. "When Is Subsidized Adoption Preferable to Long-Term Foster Care?" *Child Welfare* 50: 194-200.

Banks, Robin K., and Cappon, Daniel. "Developmental Deprivation and Mental Illness: A Study of 20 Questions." *Child Development* 34: 709-718.

Beckett, Joyce, "Casework and Psychotherapy With the Lower-Class Black Client." unpublished paper, Graduate Department of Social Work and Social Research, Bryn Mawr College, 1970.

Billingsley, Andrew. *Black Families in White America.* Englewood Cliffs, N.J.: Prentice-Hall, 1968.

_____. "Family Functioning in the Low-Income Black Community." *Social Casework* 50: 563-572.

Blau, Zena Smith. "Class Structure, Mobility and Change in Child Rearing." *Sociometry* 28: 210-219.

_____. "Exposure to Child Rearing Experts: A Structural Interpretation of Class-Color Differences." *Amer. J. Sociol.* 69: 596-608.

Bowlby, John, *et al., Maternal Care and Mental Health.* Geneva: World Health Organization, 1952.

_____. *Attachment and Loss. Vol. I: Attachment.* New York: Basic Books, 1969.

Bullough, Bonnie. "Alienation in the Ghetto." *Amer. J. Sociol.* 72: 469-478.

Calmek, Maynard. "Racial Factors in the Countertransference: The Black Therapist and the Black Client." *Amer. J. Orthopsychiat.* 40: 39-46.

Chilman, Catherine S. "Child Rearing and Family Relationship Patterns of the Very Poor." *Welfare in Review* 3: 9-19.

Coles, Robert. "It's the Same, But It's Different." *Daedalus* 94: 1107-1132.

Community Council of Greater New York. *Paths of Child Placement.* New York: Community Council of Greater New York, 1966.

Community Service Society of New York. "The Pursuit of Promise: The Intellectually Superior Child in a Deprived Area." New York: Community Service Society, April 1967 (mimeographed).

Cox, Rachel Dunaway. *Youth into Maturity.* New York: Mental Health Center Materials, 1970.

Davis, Allison, and Dollard, John. *Children of Bondage.* Washington, D.C.: American Council on Education, 1940.

Dentler, Robert A. "Barriers to Northern School Desegregation." *Daedalus* 95: 45-63.

Drake, St. Clair. "The Social and Economic Status of the Negro in the United States." *Daedalus* 94: 771-814.

Edwards, G. Franklin. "Community and Class Realities: The Ordeal of Change." *Daedalus* 95: 1-23.

Erikson, Erik H. "The Concept of Identity in Race Relations." *Daedalus* 95: 145-171.

_____. *Childhood and Society.* New York: W. W. Norton, 1950.

Emerson, Rupert, and Kilson, Martin. "The American Dilemma in a Changing World: The Rise of Africa and the Negro American." *Daedalus* 94: 1055-1084.

Fanon, Frantz. *The Wretched of the Earth.* New York: Grove Press, 1968.

Fanshel, David. *A Study in Negro Adoption.* New York: Child Welfare League of America, 1957.

Fein, Rashi. "An Economic and Social Profile of the Negro American." *Daedalus* 94: 815-846.

Fichter, Joseph H. "American Religion and the Negro." *Daedalus* 94: 1085-1106.

Filbush, Esther. "The White Worker and the Negro Client." *Social Casework* 46: 271-277.

Fischer, John H. "Race and Conciliation: The Role of the School." *Daedalus* 95: 24-44.

Fleming, Harold G. "The Federal Executive and Civil Rights: 1961-65." *Daedalus* 94: 921-948.

Foley, Eugene. "The Negro Business Man: In Search of a Tradition." *Daedalus* 95: 107-144.

Fraiberg, Selma. "Origins of Human Bonds." *Commentary* 44: 47-57.

Franklin, John Hope. "The Two Worlds of Race: A Historical View," *Daedalus* 94: 899-920.

Frazier, E. Franklin. *Black Bourgeoisie*. Glencoe, Ill.: Free Press, 1957.

———————. *The Negro in the United States*. New York: Macmillan, 1957.

Garrett, Beatrice L. "Meeting the Crisis in Foster Family Care." *Children,* Department of Health, Education and Welfare, Washington, D.C.: Government Printing Office, 1966, 3-8.

Glazer, Nathan, and Moynihan, Daniel. *Beyond the Melting Pot*. Cambridge, Mass.: M. I. T., 1963.

Gioseffi, William. "The Relationship of Culture to the Principles of Casework." *Social Casework* 32: 190-196.

Graham, Francis, *et al.* "Development Three Years after Perinatal Anoxia and Other Potentially Dangerous Newborn Experiences." *Psychol. Monog. General and Applied* 76: No. 522.

Grier, Eunice, and Grier, George. "Equality and Beyond: Housing Segregation in the Great Society." *Daedalus* 95: 77-106.

Grigg, Charles, and Killian, Lewis M. "Urban Development and Negro Home Ownership: A Case Study." Florida State University Research Report, *Social Science* 1904: 15-23.

Haitch, Richard. "Children in Limbo." *The Nation* 196: 279-281.

Hamilton, Gordon. *Theory and Practice of Social Casework*. New York: Columbia University Press, 1951.

Handel, Gerald, ed. *The Psychological Interior of the Family*. Chicago: Aldine, 1967.

Hannerz, Ulf. *Soulside Inquiries into Ghetto Culture and Community*. New York: Columbia University Press, 1969.

Hauser, Philip M. "Demographic Factors in the Integration of the Negro." *Daedalus* 94: 847-877.

Herzog, Elizabeth. "Some Assumptions about the Poor." *Social Service Review* 37: 389-402.

Hoopes, Janet L., *et al. A Followup Study of Adoptions (Vol. 2): Post-Placement Functioning of Adopted Children*. New York: Child Welfare League of America, 1969.

Hughes, Everett C. "Anomalies and Projections." *Daedalus* 94: 1133-1147.

John, Vera P. "Intellectual Development of Slum Children — Some Preliminary Findings." *Amer. J. Ortho.* 33: 813-822.

Johnson, Charles S. *Growing Up in the Black Belt*. Washington, D.C.: American Council on Education, 1941.

Kardiner, Abram, and Ovesey, Lionel. *The Mark of Oppression*. New York: W. W. Norton, 1951, 301-317.

Klein, Donald C., and Lindemann, Eric. "Preventive Intervention in Individual and Family Crisis Situations." In Gerald Caplan, ed., *Prevention of Mental Disorders in Children,* New York: Basic Books, 1961, 284.

Lawder, Elizabeth A. "Quasi-Adoption." *Meeting the Crisis in Foster Family Care.* U. S. Department of Health, Education and Welfare. Washington, D.C.: Government Printing Office, 1966.

Lawder, Elizabeth A., *et al. A Followup Study of Adoptions: Post-Placement Functioning of Adoption Families, Vol. I*. New York: Child Welfare League of America, 1969.

Lewis, Hylan. "Child-Rearing Practices Among Low-Income Families." *Casework Papers*. New York: Family Service Association of America, 1961.

Lynn, David B. *Structured Doll Play Test*. Denver: Test Developments, Box 8306, 1950.

Maas, Henry S., and Engler, Richard E. *Children in Need of Parents*. New York: Columbia University Press, 1959.

Mahn, F. Theodore. "Hiring Practices and Selection Standards in the San Francisco Bay Area." *Industrial and Labor Relations Review* 8: 231-252.

Merrill, Barbara A. "A Measurement of Mother-Child Interaction." *J. Abnorm. & Social Psychol.* 41: 37-49.

Moynihan, Daniel Patrick. "Employment, Income and the Ordeal of the Negro Family." *Daedalus* 94: 745-769.

Parsons, Talcott. "Full Citizenship for the Negro American?" *Daedalus* 94: 1009-1054.

Pasamanick, Benjamin, and Lilienfeld, A. M. "Association of Maternal and Fetal Factors With the

Development of Mental Deficiency: Abnormalities in Prenatal and Paranatal Periods." *J.A.M.A.* 159: 135-160.

Pasamanick, Benjamin, Rogers, M. E., and Lilienfeld, A. M. "Pregnancy Experience and the Development of Behavior Disorder in Children." *Amer. J. Psychiatry* 112: 613-617.

Pettigrew, Thomas F. "Complexity and Change in American Racial Patterns." *Daedalus* 94: 974-1008.

Prelinger, Ernst, and Simet, Carl N. *An Ego-Psychological Approach to Character Assessment.* Glencoe, Ill.: Free Press, 1964.

Rainwater, Lee. "Crucible of Identity." *The American Negro,* edited by Parsons and Clark. Boston: Houghton Mifflin, 1965, 66.

Richmond Area Community Council. "A Study of Substitute Care of Children." Richmond, Virginia, 1965, mimeographed.

Robinson, Halbert B. "Growing Up Replete." In Helen D. Stone, ed., *Foster Care in Question.* New York: Child Welfare League of America, 1970.

Rohrer, John, and Edmondson, Munro. *The Eighth Generation Grows Up.* New York: Harper and Row, 1960. (A followup of the Davis and Dollard study.)

Roper, Elmo. "Discrimination in Industry: Extravagant Injustice." *Industrial and Labor Relations Review* 5: 584-592.

Rosen, Bernard, and D'Andrade, Ray. "The Psychosocial Origins of Achievement Motivation." *Sociometry* 22: 185-217.

Sears, Robert, Maccoby, Eleanor, and Levin, Harry. *The Patterns of Child Rearing.* Evanston, Ill.: Row Peterson, 1957.

Spitz, Rene A. "Hospitalism: An Inquiry into the Genesis of Psychiatric Conditions in Early Childhood." In *Psychoanalytic Study of the Child, Vol. I.* New York: International Universities Press, 1945, 53-74.

Thomas, Alexander, *et al. Behavioral Individuality in Early Childhood.* New York: New York University Press, 1963.

Tobin, James. "Improving the Economic Status of the Negro." *Daedalus* 94.

Turner, John B., and Young, Whitney M., Jr. "Who Has the Revolution? or Thoughts on the Second Reconstruction." *Daedalus* 94.

U. S. Department of Labor and Department of Commerce. "The Social and Economic Status of Negroes in the United States." Washington, D.C.: Government Printing Office, 1969.

Walters, James, and Connors, Ruth. "Interaction of Mothers and Children From Lower Class Families." *Child Development* 35: 433-440.

Wilson, James Q. "The Negro in Politics." *Daedalus* 94: 949-973.

Winterbottom, Marion J. "The Relation of Childhood Training in Independence to Achievement Motivation," referred to by Irvin Child in "Socialization," in Gardner Lindzey, ed., *Handbook of Social Psychology, Vol. 2.* Cambridge, Mass.: Addison-Wesley, 1954.

Wortis, Helen, *et al.* "Child Rearing Practices in a Low Economic Group." *Pediatrics* 32: 298.

Yarrow, Marian Radke. "Problems of Methods in Parent-Child Research." *Child Development* 34: 215-226.

Zunich, Michael. "A Study of Relationships Between Child Rearing Attitudes and Maternal Behavior." *J. Exp. Educ.* 30: 231-241.

_____ . "Children's Reactions to Failure." *J. Genetic Psych.* 104: 19-24.